THE NEW ILLUSTRATED GUIDE TO

MODERN
ELITE
FORCES

SMITHMARK

THE NEW ILLUSTRATED GUIDE TO

MODERN
ELITE
FORCES

DAVID MILLER & GERARD RIDEFORT

A Salamander Book

©Salamander Books Ltd. 1992
129-137 York Way,
London N7 9LG,
United Kingdom.

ISBN 0-8317-5052-9

This edition published in 1992 by
SMITHMARK Publishers, Inc., 112
Madison Avenue, New York, NY 10016.

SMITHMARK Books are available for
bulk purchase for sales promotion and
premium use. For details write or
telephone the Manager of Special
Sales. SMITHMARK Publishers, Inc.,
112 Madison Avenue, New York,
NY 10016. (212) 532-6660.

Credits

Authors: A former serving officer in the
British Army, David Miller is now a full-
time author with a specialist
knowledge of military and technical
subject matter.

Gerard Ridefort has spent all his adult
life in military service; a career which
has included the commanding of
special forces units in Europe and the
Middle East.

Editor: Bob Munro
Designers: Phil Gorton and John
Heritage

Figure artworks: Rick Scollins
Maps and diagrams: Alan Hollingbery
and TIGA
Picture research: Tony Moore
Filmset by Modern Text Typesetting
Ltd and The Old Mill
Color reproduction by Scantrans Pte.
Printed in Hong Kong

Photographs: The publisher wishes to
thank all the official government
archives and individuals who have
supplied pictures for this book.
Photograph agencies only are credited
on the page their pictures appear.

Contents

Special Air Services

The Australian SAS Regiment was formed in July 1957 as 1st SAS Company. It was the first ever Australian special forces unit, and was clearly based upon the lessons learned in the Malayan campaign, which was then winding down. In 1960 the unit was transferred into the Royal Australian Regiment, the regular infantry element of the Australian Army. On September 4, 1964, the unit became independent again, was increased in size, and became the Australian Special Air Service Regiment.

1 SAS Squadron of the regiment deployed to Brunei in 1965 as part of the force countering Indonesian "confrontation", followed later by 2 SAS Squadron which went to Borneo. At virtually the same time Australia became involved in the Vietnam War and the three SAS squadrons rotated through that country from 1966 to 1971. They established a considerable reputation for themselves in Vietnam, serving mostly in Phuoc Tuy province to the south-east of the capital, Saigon.

The Australian SAS has not deployed operationally since the end of the Vietnam War (at least as far as public knowledge is concerned). But it is of considerable interest that, despite the very small size of the current Australian Army —they have only six regular battalions, for example—they still retain the SAS Regiment.

Organisation

At the height of the Vietnam and Confrontation campaigns the Australian SAS Regiment comprised: a headquarters; a Base Squadron; 1, 2 and 3 SAS Squadrons; and elements of 151 Signal Squadron. Since the war there has been slight reduction with the disbandment of 2 SAS Squadron; the rest remain.

Selection and training

Like the British SAS, the Australian SAS selects men from volunteers from other Army units; there is no recruiting direct from civilian life. Selection methods, too, are similar, but as there is no Australian marine corps there is a stronger emphasis on maritime activities.

Uniform

The Australian SAS Regiment personnel wear standard Australian Army uniform. Rather than the famous slouch-hat, however, they wear the equally famous sand-coloured beret and metal winged dagger badge of Britain's SAS. The wings, worn on the right sleeve, are also of the British SAS pattern.

1st Ranger Squadron, New Zealand SAS

The New Zealand Special Air Service Squadron was formed in 1954 to join the British and Rhodesian SAS in Malaya. As in Rhodesia, the initial volunteers were taken straight from civilian life and 138 were

Camouflage combat uniform

Sweatrag worn as combat hat

Bergen rucksack

Strap for canvas satchel

5.56mm M16A1 rifle

Combat knife

Pouch

M68 fragmentation grenade

Above: Australian SAS trooper on a jungle operation. He is armed with an M16A1 rifle and carries a "commando" knife.

accepted from a list of some 800. With 40 regular officers and NCOs, these were trained in New Zealand from June until November 1955 when the survivors were sent to Singapore to complete their parachute and jungle training. They soon deployed onto operations and spent 17 months out of the next two years in the jungle, killing 26 terrorists for the loss of just one of their own soldiers.

The squadron returned to New Zealand in November 1957 to be disbanded, but was resuscitated in August 1958. A troop of 30 men

Left: A New Zealand SAS troop departs from one of the Royal New Zealand Air Force's BAe Andover transport aircraft.

was sent to Korat in Thailand from May to September 1962 in support of SEATO. In 1963 the unit was redesignated 1st Ranger Squadron, New Zealand Special Air Service, and shortly afterwards the unit deployed to Borneo where it served, once again, alongside the British SAS. It also operated from time to time with the Britain's SBS. 4 Troop NZSAS served in Vietnam from November 1968 to February 1971, where it served with the Australian SAS Squadron.

The unit is now stationed near Auckland in New Zealand. It has five troops and an HQ, with a separate small training establishment. Its task is to support New Zealand defence forces in their operations and, like the SAS in the United Kingdom, it has a major commitment to counter-terrorist missions. The uniform is standard New Zealand army, but badges are similar to those of the British SAS.

Special Service Force

Canada's Special Service Force is declared to NATO and is committed to the defence of North Norway as part of the Canadian Combined Air/Sea Transportable Brigade (CAST). In Norway the CAST would operate in conjunction with other allied formations such as the British/Netherlands Amphibious Force, the USMC Marines Amphibious Force and the Norweigan Army. Within Canada the Special Service Force concentrates on operations in the far north, and produces special rescue teams to deal with civilian emergencies.

The core of the Special Service Force is the Canadian Airborne Regiment, which is the elite unit of the Canadian armed forces. The airborne regiment can trace its origins back to the 1st Canadian Parachute Battalion, which was raised at Camp Shiloh in 1942, and the 2nd Parachute Battalion which later became part of the combined US/Canadian 1st Special Service Force (from which the modern force takes its name, even though there is no US involvement). The Canadian parachute force was maintained at a low level following World War II up to 1968 when the Canadian Airborne Regiment was formed to be a light, independent infantry unit for deployment in low-intensity operations.

Organisation

The Special Service Force is organised as a light brigade, although with only two infantry units its tactical viability is open to some question. Teeth arm units are an armoured regiment (8th Canadian Hussars), an infantry battalion (1st Battalion Royal Canadian Regiment) and the Canadian Airborne Regiment. Combat support comes from an airborne artillery regiment (2nd Royal Canadian Horse Artillery), an ▶

Right: The "Skyhawks" freefall parachute team is formed from men of the Canadian Airborne Regiment. Here they move towards joining up with the team leader.

Above: Trainees for the Airborne Regiment are checked out by the jumpmaster. No. 1 Airborne Commando consists entirely of French-Canadians.

Below: Gunners of 2nd Royal Canadian Horse Artillery bring their C-5 105mm pack-how into action. This is a local version of the Oto Melara Model 56.

► engineer regiment and a signal squadron. Combat service support comes from the Airborne Service Commando (ie, logistic regiment).

The Canadian Airborne Regiment itself consists of three airborne commandos, which are equivalent to a company in size and organisation. 1st Airborne Commando is francophone (composed of French-Canadians), 2nd Airborne Commando is anglophone (English-Canadians), and 3rd is mixed.

Weapons and equipment

Small arms used by the Canadian Airborne Regiment include the US M16A1. However, there are also two Canadian adaptations of British weapons. First is the 9mm C1 sub-machine gun which is based on the Sterling L2A1, but has a simpler magazine (holding 30 as opposed to 34 rounds) and utilises the FN FAL bayonet. The most common rifle is the C1A1 7.62mm, which is modified from the L1A1

Below: Infantry soldier of the Special Service Force in winter gear. His rifle is the 7.62mm C1A1 version of the British SLR and is fitted for firing blanks.

SLR to take a magazine charger and has a rotating disc rear sight.

The Squad Automatic Weapon is the heavy-barrelled version of the FN FAL, designated the C2A1 in Canadian service. The C2A1 can be recognised by the absence of a cover over the gas cylinder and barrel and the fitting of a bipod.

Uniform

The parade uniform is the bottle-green service dress with gold stripes for officers which is common to sea, land and air elements of the Canadian Armed Forces. Combat uniform is generally of US pattern (eg, helmets) but the NCOs' badges of rank are British. One unusual feature with the airborne troops is that the parachute qualification badge is a pair of wings surmounted by a maple leaf; for those serving with the Canadian Airborne Regiment the maple leaf is white, but for all others it is red. All eligible troops wear the paratroopers' red beret.

All members of the Special Service Force wear a patch with a winged sword and the motto "Osons" ("We Dare") clearly derived from that worn by the British SAS.

11

Foreign Legion

When President Mitterand deployed a a French division to Saudi Arabia as part of Operation *Desert Shield*, it was inevitable that the Foreign Legion would provide a significant proportion of its strength. Although in the 1960s it was widely predicted that the Legion would not survive the French withdrawal from North Africa, this unique fighting force remains a key part of the French Army.

Formed in 1831, the Foreign Legion spearheaded French colonial operations during the 19th Century. Legionnaires fought in Spain, Madagascar and South-East Asia, but they were to be most closely identified with France's long-running wars in Algeria. In 1841 the Legion built a base at Sidi bel Abbes, 60 miles (96.5km) south of Oran. This was to be the spiritual home of the Legion until France granted Algeria independnece and withdrew her forces in 1962.

In 1914 much of the French Army of Africa was rushed to mainland France to stem the German invasion. Legionnaires fought with distinction throughout the ensuing holocaust on the Western Front. Indeed, by 1918 the *Régiment de Marche de la Légion Etrangère* was the most highly decorated regiment in the entire French Army.

During World War II, the Foreign Legion fought all over the world and against both sides. Some elements of the Legion fought in France and Norway in 1940 until the French surrender. Other Legionnaires left in Syria, the Lebanon and North Africa remained loyal to the Vichy regime and resisted Allied invasions.

After World War II, France tried to re-establish her authority in South-East Asia but was soon embroiled in a war with nationalist Viet Minh. One by one the garrisons were overwhelmed and Ho Chi Minh's guerrillas gained the upper hand. In 1953 the French staked everything on a decisive battle at Dien Bien Phu, only to have their 14,000-strong force surrounded and besieged. Seven Foreign Legion battalions were among the garrison that was eventually overrun by the Viet Minh in May 1954.

Of all its battles over the last 160 years, the Foreign Legion takes most pride in the last stand of an isolated company in Mexico on 30 April 1863. Refusing to surrender despite overwhelming odds, Captain Danjou's men fought practically to the last man. The anniversary — Camerone Day — is still celebrated by Legion detachments throughout the world. It is the most visible manifestation of the Legion's unique *esprit de corps*.

Organisation

The French Foreign Legion exists today as an all-arms force, well equipped (with standard French Army weapons) and well organised to serve France. Its current organisation is based on regiments of 10 companies, with the specialist companies (reconnaissance, mortar, light armour, etc) increasing at the expense of the infantry companies — a trend by no means confined to the Legion, nor indeed to the French Army. Current major units comprise:

1 er Regiment Etranger. Located at Caserne Vienot in Aubagne, this regiment is responsible for the administration of the whole Legion. It also runs the band, a company administering a large training camp, and in wartime produces three companies to defend the IRBM missile sites on the Plateau d'Albion.

2er Regiment Etranger d'Infantrie. A 1,500-strong infantry regiment based at Bonifacio, Corsica, its companies rotate through commando and other specialist schools and frequently serve on overseas detachments. ▶

Right: Kitted out for duty in a rough, hot environment, a paratrooper from the French Foreign Legion makes his way into battle. One of the most famous of the world's elite forces, it has participated in France's wars around the world for over 160 years with much distinction.

Green beret

Foreign Legion
parachute capbadge

French leather
webbing equipment

Pouch

Model 0F37
hand-grenade

Combat knife

9mm MAT 49
sub-machine gun.
Hand-grip also acts
as safety and although
his finger is on the
trigger the gun is
'safe'.

Canvas boots

13

▶ *3e Regiment Etranger d'Infantrie.*
This regiment left Malagasy in
1973 and moved to its present
base in Kourou, French Guiana.

4e Regiment Etranger. This regiment trains recruits and junior
NCOs; it is located at Castelnaudary
in France.

*1er Regiment Etranger d'Cava-
lerie.* Stationed at Orange, this
regiment is the armoured component of the French Army's 14th
Infantry Division. It consists of
three armoured car squadrons and
a lorried infantry company. It is
also earmarked as one of the
spearhead units of the French
intervention force.

*2e Regiment Etranger de Para-
chutistes.* Stationed at Corte in
Corsica, this regiment comprises

and HQ and four combat com-
panies. It prides itself in its ability to
mount an operation against any
given point in the world within 24
hours. One company is usually
detached to *13DBLE.*

5e Regiment Mixte du Pacifique.
Centred on Mururoa, the *RMP* has
detachments at Tahiti and Arue. Its
task is to provide security, communications and a power station
for the French nuclear test sites in
the Pacific. (As it includes French
Army elements the regiment is
designated *Mixte* rather than
Etranger.)

*61e Battaillon Mixte du Genie de
la Legion.* This engineer battalion
was formed to prepare training
areas, and is currently working on
an arid site known as Les Causses

Rescue at Kolwezi May 1978

Following the widespread disorders
after the granting of independence
in 1960 and the resulting United
Nations intervention, General
Mobutu became President of Zaire
in 1965. He had to deal with a
succession of outbreaks of trouble
in the following years, especially in
Shaba province, formerly Katanga,
the breakaway province once under

the leadership of Möise Tshombe.

On May 13, 1978, a force of
some 4,000 "Tigers" of the *Front
National de Liberation du Congo*
(FNLC) swept into Kolwezi, cutting
its lines of communication with the
capital, and inflicting heavy casualties on the Zairian army. There then
followed an orgy of bloodshed and
rape, and hundreds of Eruopean

Frank Spooner Pictures

in the Dordogne. The battalion comprises one Legion infantry company and one company of French Army engineers.

Detachment Legion Etrangere de Mayotte. This detachment of two companies, commanded by a lieutenant-colonel, is on the island of Mayotte in the Indian ocean. The island is a staging post on the route to Reunion and the 250-strong Legion unit guarantees its security.

Uniform

The Legion wears standard French Army uniforms, but with some special items to denote its status. The most famous item is the white-topped *kepi (kepi blanc)*, which is actually a white cloth cover on a standard blue *kepi* (with red top and gold badge and chin-strap). The *kepi blanc* cover is not worn by *sous* officers and above. Parade dress is khaki battledress with a number of ceremonial additions including green shoulder-boards with red tassels, white belt and gaiters, blue waist sash, and white gauntlets. A green tie is worn and officers also wear a green waistcoat. Members of the pioneer platoon wear a white apron and carry a ceremonial axe; they are also permitted to grow a beard.

Combat dress is the standard French camouflage suit, usually with a beret. Regiments on operations use a *foulard*, a strip of coloured cloth, to indicate companies. Foreign Legion parachutists wear the green beret.

---

men, women and children were murdered or kidnapped. On May 14 President Mobutu formally requested help from France, and to the credit of the French they responded both rapidly and effectively.

The rescue operation

On May 17, 1978, at about 1000 hours, 2nd Foreign Legion Parachute Regiment (2^eREP) at its base at Calvi in Corsica was placed at 6 hours notice to move. Executive orders did not arrive until 0130 hours the next morning and by 0800 hours the regiment was at the Solenzara airbase ready to go. The first echelon left that afternoon on five chartered DC-8 aircraft belonging to French civil airlines, to be followed later by the balance of the unit, together with the heavy weapons and vehicles, in USAF C-141s and C-5s.

The DC-8s arrived at Kinshasa airfield that evening and the legionnaires were greeted with the news that they were to emplane almost at once in four C-130 Hercules and two C-160 Transall aircraft of the Zairian air force to fly some 1,240 miles (2,000km) to Kolwezi. Their task was to carry out a "humanitarian combat mission" to rescue all civilians, of whatever race or colour, trapped in and around Kolwezi. Little firm information could be given on the situation in Kolwezi. Few of the men had ever jumped from C-130s and all would have to use American T-10 parachutes which they were not used to. The jump would be from an altitude of 650ft (200m).

The men of 2^eREP worked through the night to get organised, and were then piled somewhat haphazardly into the aircraft. The situation was exacerbated when a C-160 blew a tyre on take-off and the legionnaires were taken out of that aircraft and told to push their way into the five remaining machines. With 80 paratroops stuffed into an aircraft designed to take 66, carrying strange parachutes, after a long journey from Corsica and having had no sleep for 48 hours, plus a bumpy four-hour flight to the jump point, the situation seemed ripe for disaster. However, due to the innate good sense of the legionnaires and their sound training, all went smoothly somehow. ▶

Left: Legionnaires of 2^e REP move through the scrub near Kolwezi looking for "Tigers" or their unfortunate European victims.

FRANCE/FOREIGN LEGION

▶ The drop, 2ᵉREP's first operational jump since Dien Bien Phu, was successful, even though the pilot dropped them directly onto the objective rather than the previously selected DZ some 1,100 yards (1,000m) distant. The men had no heavy weapons, but even though there was no immediate response to their arrival they dug in rapidly. 1ᵉ Cie occupied the Lycee John Paul XXIII, 2ᵉ Cie the hospital and a workshop, and 3ᵉ Cie the Hotel Impala and an overpass.

The night passed with sporadic action and early the next morning the four C-130s and a lone C-160 arrived overhead with further men from the regiment. The commanding officer decided that the situation did not warrant the risk of a night jump and sent the aircraft off to nearby Lubumbashi. They returned at dawn and dropped the men and equipment successfully. During all this the legionnaires got on with the job of bringing order to the city, rescuing prisoners, and dealing (very firmly) with the so-called "Tigers" of the FNLC.

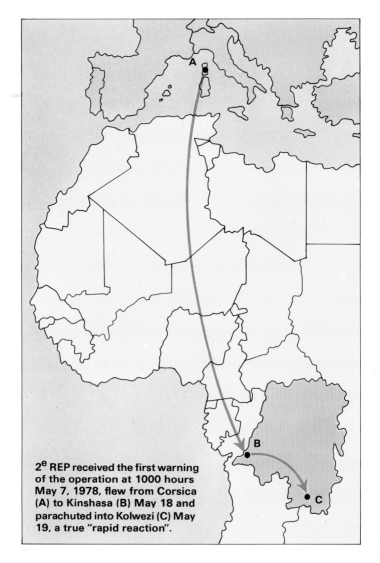

2ᵉ REP received the first warning of the operation at 1000 hours May 7, 1978, flew from Corsica (A) to Kinshasa (B) May 18 and parachuted into Kolwezi (C) May 19, a true "rapid reaction".

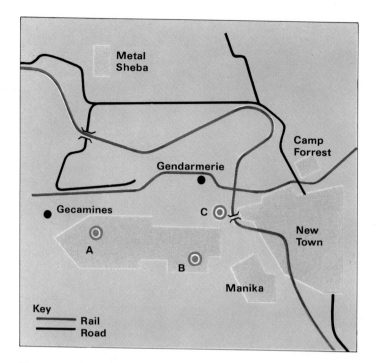

Above: When they jumped into Kolwezi, 2^e REP deployed quickly to restore order. 2^e Cie occupied the hospital (A), 1^e Cie the Lycee John Paul XXIII (B) and 3^e Cie the Hotel Impala and a road overpass (C). The operation was a great success.

Map labels: Metal Sheba · Camp Forrest · Gendarmerie · Gecamines · C · New Town · A · B · Manika

Key
— Rail
— Road

By midday May 20 (two days after the first landing) the situation in Kinshasa was sufficiently under control for 4^e Cie to move out to Metal Shaba, a township some distance to the North, where they bumped a major enemy force which put in a counter-attack against 4^e Cie, using lorryborne infantry supported by two Soviet-built light tanks. They were given short shrift by the Legion.

At first light on May 21 the majority of the regiment's transport arrived from Lubumbashi, followed in the course of the day by the remainder. Mobile at last, the companies spent the next few days scouring the countryside, looking for rebels and their prisoners. Groups of Europeans were found, half-crazed with fear as a result of their harrowing experiences with the "Tigers". A large group of rebels was totally eliminated on May 25. On May 28 2^e REP was ordered to

hand over to incoming Belgian, Moroccan and Zairian troops and move to Lubumbashi in preparation for a return to Corsica in C-141s of the USAF.

In this brief operation 2^e REP was directly responsible for saving over 3,000 Europeans and many loyal Zairians. Some 300 FNLC "Tigers" were killed and 163 captured, together with vast quantities of arms and ammunition. Five legionnaires were killed in action and 25 wounded, all by small arms fire.

The very rapid move from Corsica to Kinshasa was praiseworthy enough, but the way in which the legionnaires coped with the chaotic arrangements there and their flight to Kolwezi was quite exceptional. The unofficial Legion motto is "Demerdez vous" which literally translated means "Muddle through"; it certainly applied on this occasion.

Paratroops

The French paratroops have probably carried out more operational jumps than any other parachute corps in the world in their campaigns in Indochina, Suez (1956) and Algeria, with others since (e.g., Kolwezi). They have also at times become heavily politicised and for a few days in 1960 the inhabitants of Paris seriously expected *les paras* to drop on the capital to attempt to take over the government.

The French parachute units were among the leading units in the French campaign in Indochina and carried out some 156 operational drops. They harried the Viet Minh ruthlessly, but not without suffering heavy casualties themselves. This culminated in their jump into a small valley in the north-west corner of the country on November 21 1954, near a small village called Dien Bien Phu. Most parachute units were withdrawn and replaced by heavy infantry once the position had been secured, but when General Giap and the Viet Minh tightened the noose *les paras* returned. Five battalions jumped into the cauldron between March 13 and May 6, some on the day before the garrison fell. The paratroops and the Foreign Legion bore the brunt of the battle and fought with extreme courage—it was just that they were fighting the wrong war in the wrong place.

Following the Indochina ceasefire and the French withdrawal in 1955, the paratroop units went to Algeria, arriving just as the war there started. The paratroops had been staggered by their reverses in Indochina and by their experience in the Viet Minh prisoner-of-war camps, and they set-to to develop an entirely new code for what they saw as a crusade against the Communist-inspired guerrilla threat. They studied Mao Tse-tung's writings avidly and trained their officers and soldiers in new ways.

10th Parachute Division took time off for a brief foray in the frustrating and short-lived Suez ▶

Right: French Army "para" gets away fast from a Puma helicopter. The French were early pioneers of heliborne assault.

Below: Two generations of Vietnam warriors—a French para colonel and Lt Gen Westmoreland, later US commander in Saigon. Note French red beret, para cap-badge and para wings on right breast.

Red beret

Parachute regiment cap-badge

Ammunition belt for squad machine gun

Model OF37 hand grenade

Water bottle

7.5mm Model M1949/56 rifle

19

▶ campaign and then returned to Algeria. In January 1957 this division took over the city of Algiers which was virtually in the control of the FLN and inside two months they totally restored control. Their methods were seriously questioned, however, and there were many allegations of torture. The general frustrations of the French civilians and military in Algeria boiled over in May 1958 in an uprising which eventually led to the return of de Gaulle to the presidency. The paratroops, and in particular their General—Massu— were in the forefront of this affair. They were all also involved in the attempted *putsch* in January 1960, which was very short-lived and ended in ignominious failure.

After the Algerian war the paratroops returned to France, but the French have maintained a strong parachute capability, and have regularly used these excellent troops overseas in pursuit of French diplomatic policies. Units of what is now 11th Parachute Division have served in Zaire, Mauretania, Chad and the Lebanon, among others.

One facet of the French parachute units is the enormous influence they have had on the French Army as a whole in the post-War years. This has been due in large measure to some very powerful characters such as General Jacques Massu and General Marcel Bigeard. The latter entered the Army as a private soldier, was captured as a sergeant in the Maginot Line in 1940 and then escaped to join the Free French in England where he joined the paratroops. He was, without a doubt, one of the finest battalion commanders of his generation in any army, and his reputation was such that his return to Dien Bien Phu had an electrifying effect on the entire garrison. He went on to become a General, and arrived to inspect units by parachute, his arm at the salute as he landed in front of the honour guard.

Organisation

11th Parachute Division is based at Tarbes, although its units are somewhat scattered. It is part of the French rapid-intervention force, together with 9th Marine Light Infantry Division, 27th Alpine Division, 6th Light Armoured Division and 4th Airmobile Division. 11th Parachute Division comprises two brigades, with seven battalion-sized parachute units, one of which (1^{e}RPIMa) is under divisional control and has a para-commando/special forces role.

The other six units are: 3, 6 and 8 RPIMa equivalent to the former "colonial" paratroop units); 1 and

Below: French paras deploying from a Puma helicopter. The French have large intervention forces and have not hesitated to use them, particularly in Africa. The paras and the Foreign Legion have spearheaded such missions.

9 RCP (*chasseurs* or light infantry) and 2 REP (the Foreign Legion parachute unit). There are also two independent units: 2nd RPIMa and 13 RDP.

Selection and training

All French paratroops are volunteers and undergo the same sort of selection and training as other parachute forces. The standard of training is high and certain volunteers can go on to join one of the para-commando units (eg, 1^{e}RPIMa).

Weapons and equipment

The French paratroops are armed with the FA MAS 5.56mm assault rifle. Known as *le Clairon* (the bugle) because of its unique shape — the carrying handle extends almost the full length of the weapon — it has an integral bipod and a 25-round magazine. Designed and manufactured by the St. Etienne arsenal, it is a bullpup design ideal for paratroopers because it offers a reasonable barrel length in a short and handy weapon. It is robust and accurate to modern battlefield ranges. Its automatic fire capability finally removed the need for a sub-

Above: French Paras in Beirut in 1982. Their ill-conceived peace-keeping mission was to end in tragedy, with many killed as a result of a huge terrorist bomb explosion. Of note in this photograph are the large shoulder patches worn by each paratrooper as a means of national identity.

machine-gun, and the famous MAT-49, carried by the paras in Indo-China and Algeria, has passed out of service.

For longer range fire, the paras have the 7.62mm FR F1 sniper rifle and the elderly AA52 general-purpose machine-gun, which is overdue for replacement. The paras are well equipped with modern anti-tank weapons, from shoulder-fired rockets to the deadly MILAN wire-guided missile.

Uniforms

French paratroops wear standard French Army uniforms. Their parachute status is indicated by their red beret (except for Foreign Legion paras who wear a green beret). Para wings are large and in silver, and are worn on the right breast.

21

Parachute Regiment

The parachute units of the Indian Army are among the oldest airborne units. The first Indian parachute unit was authorised on May 15, 1941, and by October 1941 50th Indian Parachute Brigade had been formed, comprising 152nd Parachute Battalion (Indian), 151st Parachute Battalion (British) and 153rd Parachute Battalion (Gurkha).

In 1944 it was decided to form a division (44th Indian Parachute Division) and at the same time the formation of the Indian Parachute Regiment as a separate entity was authorised. The partition of the British Indian Empire in 1947 led to the split of the parachute units between India and the newly-created Pakistan. 50th Indian Parachute Brigade was quickly involved in operations in Kashmir 1947-49.

During the 1965 Indo-Pakistan operations a special independent force of commandos was raised and on July 1, 1966, the 9th Parachute Battalion was formed to take on the task, absorbing the smaller commando force in the process. A year later part of 9th Battalion was hived off to form 10th Battalion, each with three company-sized sub-units designated "groups". In 1969 both units added the suffix "commando" to their titles, becoming 9th and 10th Commandos respectively.

Organisation

The Indian Army today has eight parachute battalions, organised into two independent brigades: 50th and 51st. Both brigades have parachute-trained units and sub-units of supporting arms and services—for example, artillery, engineers, signals. 9th and 10th Para Commandos are also still part of the Indian Army order of battle, operating, as all such special forces units do, in an independent role.

Selection and training

All Indian paratroops and para-commandos are volunteers; some enter the regiments direct from civil life, while others transfer in from Regular Army units. There is a probationary period of thirty days when the men undergo various physical and mental tests, during which many are weeded out. Those who pass are sent to the Paratroopers Training School at Agra, where five jumps, including one at night, entitle the trainee to wear the coveted wings and the maroon beret. Paracommandos undergo more specialised training to suit them for their role.

Weapons and equipment

Standard sub-machine gun of India's Army, including the paratroops, is the locally-produced version of the British L2A3 Sterling 9mm. There have been reports that the L34A1 silenced version may be in service in small numbers with the para-commandos. The current rifle is again a locally-produced version of a foreign weapon. This is the Belgian FN 7.62mm FAL, which is made in India at Ishapore. The light machine-gun is the very popular and successful British L4A4, the 7.62mm conversion of the old 0.303in Bren.

Uniforms

The maroon (red) beret has been the headgear of the Indian Parachute Regiment since its inception on March 1, 1945. The capbadge at that time was identical with that of the British Parachute Regiment, except that the word "INDIA" was inscribed at the base of the parachute. This badge was retained through the early years of independence and was changed to the present design—a fully opened parachute on two symbolic wings with an upright bayonet—in 1950. The paracommandos wear the red beret, but their capbadge is a winged dagger above a scroll, all bearing a more than passing resemblance to the capbadge of the British SAS.

Right: This Indian soldier wears the coveted cap badge of one of the oldest para units in any army, raised on May 15, 1941.

Red beret

Regimental cap-badge

Parachute smock similar to British "Dennison" smock

Ammunition pouch

7.62mm FN FAL rifle, manufactured in India

Green denim trousers

Cloth puttees

Paratroops

Of all the world's elite paratroop units none has seen so much or so frequent action as those of the Israeli Defence Forces (IDF). Founded in 1948, during the War of Independence, the initial material assets were one dilapidated Curtiss C-46 Commando aircraft and 4,000 second-hand parachutes which had been bought as scrap to make silk shirts! The unit consisted of a mixture of Israeli veterans of the British Army and the Palmach, graduates of a parachute course held in Czechoslovakia, Resistance veterans, ghetto survivors and a number of adventurers.

Training was inadequate and as there were no reserve 'chutes jumps periodically ended in tragedy. The units saw little action in the war and in 1949 a new commander raised standards considerably.

Meanwhile, in the early 1950s frequent infiltration by Arab terrorists led to the formation of a small unit of high quality soldiers for reprisal operations. Named "the 101st", this was very successful, but after a few years it was amalgamated with the Paratroop Unit. After some successful actions in 1954/55 the paratroopers were expanded to brigade strength and

in 1955-56 some very effective reprisal operations were carried out. In the 1956 war the Sinai campaign opened with a drop by a parachute battalion on the Mitla Pass, with the balance of the brigade being responsible for joining up with it by road, an operation which took just 28 hours to achieve. In the battles in and around the Mitla Pass the Israeli paratroops lost 38 dead and over 100 wounded, but the Egyptians lost over 260.

In a second operation a battalion was dropped at At-Tur, on the south-eastern shore of the Gulf of Suez, with the remainder of the brigade again responsible for relieving its own isolated battalion. This done, the whole brigade then moved on to join 9th Infantry ▶

Right: Israeli paratroop on the Entebbe raid stands clear of a deliberate explosion. He carries a Soviet AK-47 rifle, of which the Israelis have vast stocks.

Below: More conventionally clad Israeli paratroops "somewhere in Lebanon". They are armed with the 5.56mm SAR Galil rifle, designed and produced in Israel.

Note:
no helmet

Two magazines
strapped back-to-
back for quick
change in action

Israeli
webbing
equipment

Captured
Soviet AK-47
assault
rifle

Magazine
pouch

Water
bottle

Israeli
combat
uniform

▶ Brigade in the capture of Sharm-el-Sheikh.

After more years of reprisal raids the Paratroops played a leading role in the 1967 Six-Day War. They were involved in operations at Gaza and on the Suez Canal, but their greatest moment came when they achieved the goal of every Israeli by recapturing the Old City of Jerusalem on June 7, 1967. This battle involved taking great care to ensure that there was no damage to the holiest shrines of three major religions, which inevitably meant that the paratroops took more casualties than normal.

After the war more raids were undertaken, including those against the PLO HQ in Jordan (March 21, 1968, 250 enemy killed), the capture and return to Israel of a complete Soviet radar installation (December 23, 1969), the destruction of Arab aircraft at Beirut airport (December 12, 1968) and the rescue of hostages in a hijacked Sabena aircraft at Lod Airport (May 12, 1972).

In the Yom Kippur war the paratroopers did not undertake any parachute operations, but were involved in some desperate fighting, first to hold back the Egyptian attack and then to turn the tables by both containing enemy troops on the west bank of the canal and by crossing the canal itself into Egyptian home territory.

In July 1976 the paratroops provided the men for the raid on Entebbe where they lost their commanding officer—Lieutenant Colonel "Yoni" Netanyahu, leading his men, as always, from the front. Since then the paratroops have been involved in more fighting, particularly in the Lebanon.

Organisation

There are five parachute brigades in the IDF. Two of these are normally at, or very near, full strength; one is well above 50 per cent; and two are at cadre strength. The IDF's very efficient call-out and training system ensures that units depending upon reservists for achieving war strength are reinforced very quickly, indeed.

Below: Paratroops are inherently flexible. These Israeli paras are disembarking from a tank-landing ship mounted in M113 armoured personnel carriers on an operation in the Lebanon.

Right: Israeli paratroops on parade; note the red berets and parachute wings on the left breast. The corporal nearest the camera carries an UZI 9mm SMG, widely used by parachute forces.

Selection and training

All fit males in Israel must perform three years of military service, and all may volunteer for the parachute troops. Selection and training are rigorous, and emphasise practical military skills such as weapon training, demolitions, covert cross-border operations and field medicine. The physical requirements are very tough. All must obviously qualify as parachutists and many then go on to specialise in HALO techniques. Night operations and helicopter assault are regularly practised. ▶

Right: Israeli paratrooper at the ready. He carries the 7.62mm ARM Galil assault rifle. This version has a carrying-handle, a bipod (folded under the barrel), and a folding stock.

▶ Weapons and equipment

Like other units of the IDF the paratroops use Israeli weapons and equipment wherever possible, but supplemented with either purchased items of Western origin or captured items (usually, but not always, of Eastern origin). Parachutes are American, but small arms are Israeli. For many years the Israeli paratroops have used the Uzi sub-machine gun, but this is now being replaced by the Galil SAR rifle, an Israeli-designed and produced 5.56mm weapon with a 35-round magazine. An extremely robust and reliable weapon, the Galil incorporates the lessons learned in Israel's continuous conflicts of the past 35 years. Its advantages to the paratroops, in comparison with the Uzi, are that it provides greater range, hitting power and penetration.

Uniforms

IDF paratroopers wear standard Israeli uniforms and helmets. The customary parachutist's red beret is worn when the glassfibre combat helmet is not required. The parachutist's badge is in silver and is worn on the left breast above campaign medals.

269 Counterterrorist Unit

The existence of a special group within the IDF parachute troops has been reported from time to time. Designated 269 Counterterrorist Unit this is said to be the unit which provided the men for the raid on Entebbe. If these reports are correct it can be presumed that the unit is a specially trained and equipped group at a high state of readiness, and akin to West Germany's GSG 9 in function.

Right: Israeli frogman on the shoreline aims his Galil assault rifle, resting the bipod on a rock to steady his aim. The Galil is modelled in some respects on the Soviet AK-47 series, but also incorporates the lessons of 50 years of warfare in Israel.

Operation Jonathan Entebbe Rescue 3/4 July 1976

At 0900 hours June 27, 1976, Air France flight AF 139 left Tel Aviv airport en route for Paris. The A-300 Airbus aircraft staged through Athens and it was on the second leg of its flight when, at 1210 hours, it was skyjacked by seven Palestinian terrorists led by a German called Boese. The pilot succeeded in pressing the "hijack button" as he turned for Benghazi, where, after a 6½ hour delay, the plane was refuelled; it then flew on to the terrorists' destination— Entebbe in Uganda, which was under the erratic rule of "Field Marshal" Idi Amin Dada.

Amin endeavoured to maintain a neutral posture, but covertly he supported the terrorists in their demands that unless Palestinian prisoners held in a number of countries were released the hostages would be shot at 1200 hours on July 1. Ugandan troops were deployed at Entebbe airport, supposedly to "keep the peace", but they were in fact assisting in guarding the hostages. Amin even visited the hostages and after he had left the Israelis and Jews of other nationalities were segregated, although the entire Air France aircrew insisted on joining them.

On the morning of July 1 the Isaelis, playing for time, announced that they were willing to consider the release of Palestinian prisoners. The hijackers, increasingly confident of eventual success, responded by extending their deadline by three days. They also released all the non-Jewish hostages, who were flown to Paris, where they were given detailed debriefing by French and Israeli intelligence.

The Israeli planners had many problems. The first clearly was shortage of time: time to achieve something before the terrorists killed any of their hostages and time to set up a rescue attempt. The second was to find out just where the hostages were being held and under what conditions. Third, there was the problem of ▶

getting a rescue force all the way to Entebbe and back with the rescued hostages. Fourth, there was the problem of what to do with the non-Jewish hostages.

Fortunately, the problems re-

Above: A scene from the EMI film "Operation Thunderbolt" showing the staff planners with a detailed model of the airfield at Entebbe. (No photographs of the rescue were released.)

29

▶ solved themselves one after another. The Kenya government agreed to the use of Nairobi airport, and a coup in Sudan resulted in the closure of all but one of that country's air control radars. Intelligence on Entebbe Airport and the local situation began to be processed in, aided considerably by the debriefing of the released non-Jewish hostages. This also removed the problem of consulting foreign governments, except that of France who remained involved not only because it had been an Air France airliner that was hijacked in the first place, but also because the courageous crew insisted on staying with the Jewish hostages.

The Rescue

Lieutenant-General Mordecai Gur, Israeli chief-of-staff, considered that a raid on the airport was feasible and at 0730 hours on July 3 Prime Minister Rabin reviewed all the facts and then gave the political go-ahead for the operation. Later that morning a full-scale dress rehearsal was held in northern Israel. The force, commanded by Brigadier-General Dan Shomron, aged 48, performed well in an attack on a dummy layout manned by Israeli troops, and all seemed to augur well for the real thing, which was scheduled for the next day. The dress rehearsal lasted just 55 minutes from the time the aircraft

EMI

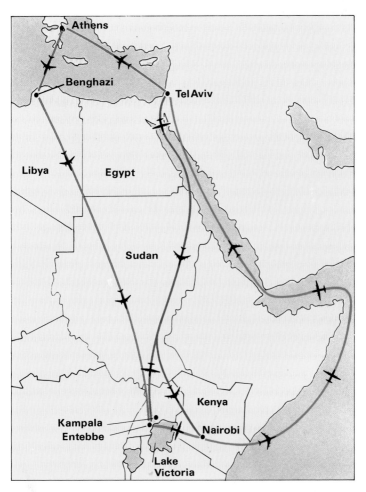

Above: Flight AF 139 (red) was hijacked on leaving Athens and taken via Benghazi to Entebbe. The rescuers flew in two groups (blue). Four C-130s refuelled at Eilat and then flew down the Red Sea, along the Sudan-Ethiopia border and into Entebbe. The other group (two Boeing 707s) followed, one circling Entebbe as a command post, the other a medical aircraft going to Nairobi. The rescuers returned (green) via Nairobi to a heroes' welcome.

Left: Another scene from the film, with Israeli paratroops relaxing in the hold of a C-130 transport aircraft on the long, hazardous flight to Entebbe.

landed to the time they took off again. The force to enter the airport terminal and rescue the hostages was to be led by Lieutenant-Colonel Jonathan Netanyahu, known throughout the Israeli Army as "Yoni". Shomron, an experienced paratrooper, had led several penetration raids into Egypt, and had been commanding officer of the first infantry battalion to reach the Suez Canal in the 1967 Arab-Israeli War. Netanyahu was nine years younger and had already been decorated for bravery, and was a very popular officer.

At 1600 hours that afternoon (July 3), only two hours after the full Israeli cabinet had been made aware of the "go" decision, four ▶

EMI

▶ C-130 Hercules aircraft of the Israeli Air Force took off for the long flight to Entebbe. The route took them down the middle of the Red Sea at high altitude in the hope that Saudi Arabian radars would treat them as unscheduled civil flights. There was, in fact, no response, so they were able to turn and fly down the Sudan-Ethiopia border and into Uganda.

Two Boeing 707s were also involved, leaving two hours after the slower C-130s. One was a flying command-post fitted with special communications; it caught up with the four C-130s near Entebbe and remained in the area throughout the operation with Major Generals Benny Peled and Yekutiel Adam aboard. The other 707, fitted out as an emergency hospital, went straight to Nairobi, arriving just before midnight; it then waited, its medical staff ready for any wounded from the operation across the border in Uganda.

The four C-130s arrived at Entebbe without incident and landed at precisely 0001 hours. The first aircraft landed close to the control-tower disgorging its paratroops in a Mercedes car and three Land Rovers while still moving. The men charged into the tower and succeeded in preventing the controllers from switching off the landing lights; even so, emergency lights were deployed, just in case. These were not needed and the second and third aircraft taxied up to the terminal where the hostages were being held and discharged their

Above: Israeli paratroops pour into the Entebbe airport building where the hostages are being held (a filmed reconstruction).

paratroopers straight into action. The fourth C-130 joined the first near the control tower.

The main Israeli squad brushed aside the slight and ineffective resistance from the Ugandan Army guards, killing some twenty in the process, and charged into the terminal building. The second group went off to destroy as many as possible of the Ugandan Air Force MiG-15, -17 and -21 jet fighters standing on the runway; this served both to prevent pursuit when the raiders took off again and also as a noisy and obvious diversion.

The third group went to the perimeter to cover the approach road since it was known that the Ugandan Army had a number of Soviet-built T-54 tanks and Czech OT-64 armoured personnel carriers some 20 miles (32km) away in the capital, Kampala. Had this force appeared it could have had a major effect as the Israelis had no heavy weapons; fortunately, nothing happened. The fourth group was made up of 33 doctors who, being Israelis, were also well-trained soldiers and brought down covering fire from the area of the C-130s.

With Shomron in control in the tower and satisfied that the first phase had been successful it was now "Yoni" Netanyahu's turn to lead the crucial assault on the terminal building to rescue the hostages. The terrorist leader, Wilfried Boese, behaved with surprising indecision, first aiming at the hostages and then changing his mind, going outside, loosing off a few rounds at the Israelis and then heading back for the lounge; as he returned he was shot and killed. His fellow German, Gabrielle Tiedemann, was also killed outside the building.

The Israeli soldiers rushed into the lounge where the hostages were being held, shouting at everyone to get down on the floor; in the confusion three of the hostages were shot by stray bullets, an almost inevitable consequence in such a situation. While some of the soldiers rushed upstairs to kill the two terrorists remaining there, the hostages were shepherded out to the waiting C-130s. At this point "Yoni" Netanyahu emerged from the terminal to supervise the loading and was killed by one shot from a Ugandan solider in a nearby building, a sad loss.

At 0045 hours the defensive outposts were called in as the first C-130 roared off into the night with its load of rescued hostages on their way to Nairobi, with the fourth and last leaving at 0054.

The whole operation had taken just 53 minutes, two minutes less than the rehearsal.

The Israelis lost Colonel Netanyahu killed and three men wounded. Three hostages were killed in the rescue, while a fourth, Mrs Dora Bloch, who had been taken off to a local hospital earlier, was murdered by the Ugandans in revenge for the raid.

The whole operation was a brilliant success, mounted at short notice and in a most unexpected direction. It confirmed the Israeli reputation for quick and determined "ad hoc" actions, conducted with great dedication and skill. The Ugandans could not be described as substantial foes, but the terrorists had obviously been trained for their task. Interestingly, it later became known that Colonel Ulrich Wegener of GSG 9 was with the Israelis on the operation, possibly because of the known presence of the two Germans with the terrorists.

Below: Israeli rescuer in the assault on the Entebbe airport building. He is armed with a 9mm UZI sub-machine gun, standard issue to all Israeli forces.

EMI

ITALY

Alpine Troops

The major land threat to Italy comes from the North and North-east, and virtually the whole of this strategically critical region is mountainous. For this reason the Italian Army has long maintained its units of crack mountain troops—the famous Alpini. There are five mountain brigades (*brigata alpina*): Taurinese, Orobica, Tridentia, Cadore and Julia. These serve in three army corps: III Corps (HQ at Milan) includes one mountain brigade; IV Corps (Bolzano) is

responsible for the defence of the crucial Brenner Pass and has three mountain brigades; and V Corps (Vittorio Veneto) is responsible for the north-eastern border with Austria and Jugoslavia, and has one mountain brigade; finally, one Alpini battalion is permanently assigned to the Allied Command Europe Mobile Force (Land).

Mountain brigades' major combat elements are one mountain infantry regiment of three or four Alpini battalions and an independent APC

4

company, and an Alpini artillery regiment with three battalions of 105mm pack-howitzers and one battalion of 155mm towed howitzers. There are also a fortress battalion, a parachute-ski platoon, a carabinieri platoon, a signal company and an engineer company. Last, but by no means least, is the logistics regiment, whose basic means of transportation is mules.

The Italian Army is due to decrease in size in the near future to reduce personnel costs and increase the amount of finance available for equipment. Although the number of brigades is due to reduce from 36 to 24 it is significant that there is to be no reduction in either the Alpine or parachute brigades. ▶

Below: Light machine gun team of an Alpini unit. Their weapon is the 7.62mm MG42/59 made in Italy by Beretta under licence from Rheinmetall. Note national flash on soldiers' left shoulder.

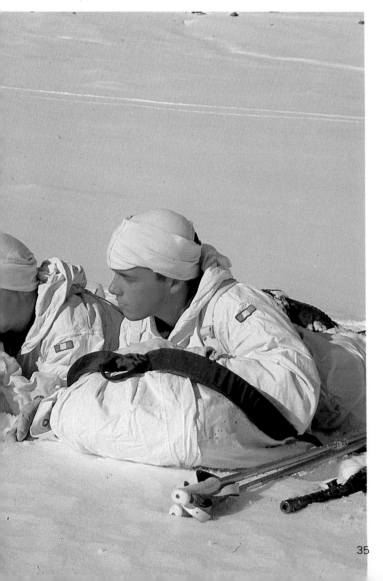

▶ Selection and training

The 2nd Alpine Regiment is responsible for basic training and there is also an Alpine warfare school. All soldiers in the mountain brigades must be trained in mountain warfare, which requires a very high standard of fitness and determination. The Italian Army as a whole has a major training problem, however, because it is made up of conscripts who serve only for twelve months, of which the first three are devoted to basic training. Add in specialist training and there is not much time left for service with a combat unit.

Weapons and equipment

The Italian army is now replacing its Beretta BM59 7.62mm rifles with the AR70/90 5.56mm assault rifle. With a 30-round magazine and fully-automatic capability, this is a modernized version of the Beretta AR70 which has been issued to some specialist units of the Italian armed forces since the late-1970s.

Right: Alpini soldier in a good firing position with his MILAN anti-tank missile. Note the snow shoe to the left of the tree; despite the legends these are of practical use to the wearer only over short distances.

Below: Italian Alpini being towed by a Norwegian Army oversnow vehicle on an Allied Mobile Force (Land) (AMF(L)) exercise in Norway. The AMF(L) is a vital NATO force under SACEUR's direct command in peace and would be the first to deploy in the event of escalating tension.

In the extreme conditions encountered in the mountains, the original AR70 was liable to damage — the pressed-steel receiver could be dented or bent out of alignment. The AR70/90 is a more robust weapon, able to keep functioning in the worst of conditions.

Support weapons for the Alpine troops include MILAN anti-tank missiles, the Folgore 80mm anti-tank rocket launcher and the OTO-Melara 105mm pack howitzer. The French Brandt light 81mm mortar is also employed; OTO-Melara manufactures the ammunition.

Uniform

The most instantly recognisable feature of Alpini dress is the famous grey-green felt mountaineers' hat, with a black eagle feather and red pompom on the left-hand side. The cap badge is of black metal and depicts an eagle above a light-infantry bugle containing the regimental number. The eagle feather and pompom are also worn on the steel helmet. The Alpini collar-patch is green. In parade dress the officers wear the traditional blue sash.

There are various types of combat dress, varying from standard combat uniform to full mountain gear of white hooded overall and trousers with a white-covered steel helmet.

San Marco Marines

The Multinational peace-keeping force in the Lebanon from 1982 to 1984 was not, in general terms, a great success, and certainly failed to fulfil its political aims. The individual military contingents did, however, conduct themselves well and one in particular that earned considerable praise was that from Italy, which was provided by the San Marco battalion of the Italian Marines, one of the elite units of the Italian Armed Forces.

The San Marco battalion is the major combat element of the 1,000 strong Italian Marines, and its men are trained in the full range of marine duties, especially amphibious warfare. They are also all parachute trained. Their mission is to provide an amphibious capability (albeit, in view of their size, a limited one) in support of the Italian and NATO fleets in the Mediterranean.

Organisation

The San Marco battalion is divided into three components: the Operational Group of four companies; the Logistics Group and the Training Group. Battalion sea transport is provided by two ex-USN Landing Ships Tank (LST), the *Caorle* (ex-USS *York County*) and the *Grado* (ex-USS *De Soto County*). So important and successful is the battalion, however, that the Italian Navy is planning under the 1975 Naval Law to build a new ship, a Landing Platform Dock (LPD) of 7,667 tons, which will have a large flight-deck for helicopters as well as a tank/vehicle deck and roll-on/roll-off facilities. Some doubts about the need for such a specialised and expensive ship have been removed by the San Marco deployment to Lebanon, and it will now be commissioned by the end of 1967.

Fighting vehicles of the battalion ▶

Above: San Marco marines
going ashore in MTP 9733, an
Italian-built landing-craft. The
San Marco battalion is Italy's
only marine unit.

Below: San Marco marines
storm ashore under the setting
sun. Their weapons are the latest
5.56mm Beretta SC70 assault
rifles with tubular folding butts.

BIGHI (SMM—UDAP)

39

Above: A squad of San Marco marines ready for an operation. Note the unique camouflage colours on the combat uniforms.

Below: 81mm mortar team leads a beach landing from LCVPs. The San Marco use few specialised weapons (see text).

include the M113A1 armoured personnel carrier, 10 LVTP-7 amphibious landing vehicles and 30 VCC-1, an Italian-produced improved version of the M113, which it is replacing.

Weapons and equipment

The San Marco Battalion was one of the specialist units to be issued with the Beretta AR70 5.56mm rifle. They trialled both the standard weapon and the SC70 version which has a folding butt. Now the entire Italian army is adopting the AR70/90 (see Alpini entry).

Otherwise, the San Marco battalion is equipped with standard Italian army weapons — the Beretta PM12 9mm sub-machine-gun; Beretta 9mm pistol and the 7.62mm MG42/59 general-purpose machine-gun. The latter is the modern version of the famous German World War II weapon built under license from Rheinmetall. The rate-of-fire is reduced but otherwise it is practically identical to the German Army's MG3.

Uniform

San Marco marines wear the usual, and easily recognisable, Italian camouflage suit, and the steel helmet whose design has not changed in forty years. A black beret is worn and the San Marco lion badge, gold on a red backing, is worn on the right sleeve cuff.

In combat order the San Marco marines dress as soldiers, but in parade order they wear naval uniform, with the embellishment of the San Marco lion badge, worn by officers on the left breast above the medal ribbons and by marines on the tunic shirt cuffs. This curious mixing of uniforms is unique.

Special Forces

A company of paratroopers was raised in 1963 and, having quickly proved its value, this has been expanded over the years until today there are three battalions of commando/paratroops, now retitled the Jordanian Special Forces. These units have taken part in numerous operations in the various Middle East wars, and have also been heavily involved during peacetime in keeping control of their troubled country. They played a leading part in the operations to suppress and finally expel the Palestine Liberation Army (PLO) commandos in 1970-71,and also retook the Inter-Continental Hotel in Amman in 1976.

Such is the reputation of the Special Forces that in 1983 the US military authorities suggested that the force be expanded to two-brigade size and used to help cope with the security problems in the Persian Gulf. This somewhat naive proposal was very complimentary to the Jordanian Special Forces, but has fortunately been dropped, as its effect both internationally and domestically within Jordan would be catastrophic.

Organisation

The three commando/paratroop battalions are organised on standard Jordanian Army lines with three companies, each of three platoons. Battalions are approximately 500 strong.

Selection and training

Members of the Jordanian Special Forces are all volunteers. They must be Bedouins with personal tribal links to King Hussein, and a proven record of undoubted loyalty. Training is the toughest in an army noted for its high standards and all men are trained in parachute, guerrilla and sabotage techniques.

Weapons and equipment

The three Special Forces battalions are equipped as light infantry, with weapons such as Dragon anti-tank guided missiles, 106mm recoilless rifles, mortars and small arms (M16 rifle, M60 MG, etc). Land transport is based on the usual jeeps and trucks. Air mobility is provided by the Royal Jordanian Air Force whose transport fleet includes: 15 Alouette III and two S-76 helicopters (with four more S-76 on order), three C-130 Hercules, and four Casa C-212 Aviocars.

Uniform

As with the rest of the army, the Jordanian Special Forces' uniform shows both British and United States' influence. US-style leaf-pattern camouflage suits are worn and most items of personal equipment are of US origin. Parachute wings are worn on the left breast and the major visible mark is the maroon beret, but worn with the standard national cap-badge. The Special Forces' badge is a white bayonet surrounded by symbolic yellow wings and surmounted by a Hashemite crown; this is backed by a maroon shield and worn on the right upper sleeve.

Right and below: Members of Jordan's elite Special Forces formation, with M16 rifle and US-style combat dress. Jordan's Army is one of the best in the Middle East. Jordan Special Forces were proposed by the Pentagon as the basis for a "fire-brigade" force in the Middle East.

Helmet with
camouflage cover

US Army temperate
climate camouflaged
combat uniform

5.56mm
M16A1 rifle

Ammunition
pouches

M61 delay
fragmentation
grenade

Respiration
bag

43

Special Forces

The forces of the Democratic Republic of Korea (North) invaded the Republic of Korea (South) (ROK) on June 25, 1950. The resulting war pulled in the Republic of China on the side of the North, and 16 nations (including the USA) on the ROK side. An armistice (not a peace treaty) was signed on July 27, 1953, and an uneasy "peace" has continued since.

Currently stationed in South Korea is the United States 8th Army, comprising 2nd Infantry Division, 19th Support Command, at least one wing of the USAF and numerous supporting units. The ROK Army comprises five corps, with one mechanised and 20 infantry divisions, two armoured brigades and a host of minor units. It also includes seven Special Forces brigades.

In contrast, the army of North Korea comprises eight corps, with two tank divisions, three motorised infantry divisions, 35 infantry divisions and the usual supporting elements. Included in these massive forces in the North are no fewer than 22 Special Forces (or commando) brigades. The North Koreans have built up sufficient forces in the central part of their territory to launch a deep and sudden attack, without help from either the USSR or PRC, which would threaten Seoul, only some 28 miles (45km) south of the DMZ. Such an attack could be facilitated by the tunnels which have been dug from time to time. One (the third) was discovered on December 27, 1978, and was 6.6ft (2m) square, quite large enough for small vehicles and light ▶

Above: All members of the South Korean Special Forces must reach black belt standard in Tae-Kwon-Do or a similar martial art; there is 4-5 hours practice daily.

Below: Soldiers of a Special Forces unit coming ashore in an inflatable boat. Rifles are US M16A1 5.56mm, but its successor will be a Korean design.

▶ guns. The Communist Special Forces brigades could use such tunnels or deploy by air or sea.

The ROK has seven Special Forces brigades organised on the same lines as US Special Forces groups, with whom there is a close working relationship. The battalions of these brigades are often used in the Ranger role for the destruction of tactical targets. These ROK Special Forces units are capable of using either continuous guerrilla operations from bases within enemy territory, or carrying out single operations from bases within friendly territory. The usual allocation of the Special Forces is one battalion to each army corps.

Selection and training

Following the usual physical and psychological tests, the volunteer undergoes a hard training course which includes weapon handling skills to a very high standard and parachute training. All ROK Special Forces troops must also reach black belt standard in Tae-Kwon-Do or a similar martial art, and when not on operations some four to five hours a day are spent in practice of such arts.

Weapons and equipment

Standard sub machine-gun in use by the Korean special forces is the US-supplied 0.45 M3A1, although this must be due for replacement by a more modern and effective weapon in the near future. The rifle of the South Korean Army is the M16A1, locally manufactured, and the squad machine-gun is the 7.62mm M60. The South Koreans are, however, taking steps to become more independent in the arms field—they have recently produced a prototype of their first ever tank design—and can therefore be considered likely to produce their own small arms, also.

Uniform

Normal uniform is a camouflage combat suit. The Special Forces distinguishing mark is a black beret with the SF badge in silver. Weapons and personal equipment are all of US origin. Pocket patches are sometimes worn, with different badges for each SF brigade.

Below: Special Forces troops on winter warfare training, firing M16A1 rifles from rests made from ski sticks. Korean winters are very severe, as the UN forces found out in 1950 to 1953.

Right: Special Forces troops climb a rock face, having come ashore from canoes. Weapon is 9mm Mini UZI SMG. Israeli-designed for police and special forces, it weighs 5.9lb (2.7kg).

44th Parachute Brigade

The South African Parachute Brigade is one of the most experienced combat units in the world today. The "Parabats" played a key role in the long-running war in Namibia/South-West Africa which began during the mid-1960s and was finally ended in March 1990. South Africa's airborne forces undertook countless operations against the SWAPO guerrillas within Namibia and also participated in a series of major assaults on SWAPO military bases inside Communist-controlled Angola.

South Africa had no paratroop forces during World War II and the decision to create an airborne unit was not taken until the late-1950s. The Nationalist Government elected in 1948 included many politicians who had opposed the country's participation in World War II; consequently, spending on defence was accorded a low priority, until it began to realise the danger from South Africa's growing isolation. As African countries began to achieve independence from European colonial powers, the need for military modernisation became clear. Airborne forces were an obvious requirement in such a vast operational area and a small team of South Africans were sent to the UK for airborne training.

As this 15-man team returned to South Africa in 1960, the country withdrew from the Commonwealth and military assistance from the UK was cut off. The promised training equipment could no longer be delivered so the South Africans had to build their own. They did not have

the exact specifications and had to rely on memory and the snapshots some of them had taken during the training course! This imposed obvious delays on the training programme and it took years to develop the facilities and experience to produce an airborne combat unit. The 1st Parachute Battalion was not formally created until April 1968.

In 1975 Portugal granted independence to Angola after many years of war with several guerrilla movements. Civil war followed as rival guerrilla armies fought for control of the country; feeble Western reaction allowed victory to go to the communist MPLA which received large arms shipments from the Soviet Union and military support from the Cuban army. This was a disaster for South Africa; the SWAPO guerrillas now had a secure base inside Angola from which they could launch attacks into Namibia.

Above: Self-sufficiency in the bush is a vital skill learnt early in training by every "Parabat". Here, one of South Africa's elite troops conducts a rudimentary snare.

Left: The "Parabats'" ability to parachute into hostile territory proved invaluable during the long-running conflict with the guerrilla forces of SWAPO.

The value of airborne forces in defeating guerrilla incursions had already been demonstrated a few years earlier. A large SWAPO raiding force was spotted on the move in northern Namibia and two companies of Parabats were flown 1,250 miles (2,000km) from Bloemfontein to make a combat jump nearby. The guerrillas fled. During the 1970s the South African airborne forces were expanded, a second and later a third battalion being created as the war in Namibia continued. South African officers were frequently seconded to the Rhodesian army which was also engaged in a death struggle with communist-backed guerrillas. The Rhodesians also had the problem of defending a large area with only a small number of soldiers and their "Fireforce" tactics were studied with ▶

Above: A two-man "Parabat" recce team on patrol. Physical strength is all-important if these troops are to carry weighty back-packs up and into mountainous terrain on long-range missions.

▶ interest by the Parabats. The Rhodesians employed quick-reaction forces in helicopters plus paratroops in ageing C-47 Dakotas. When a guerrilla unit was spotted by patrols or observation posts, the Fireforce would fly in and land enough soldiers to overwhelm and destroy the enemy before they could escape.

With more and better helicopters and aircraft at their disposal, the South Africans were even more successful in their use of airmobile troops. Most actions were platoon or company-sized operations against handfuls of elusive guerrillas; SWAPO had lost heavily every time it concentrated its forces inside Namibia and it relied on hit-and-run raids by a few individuals to intimidate the local population.

In 1978 over 300 Parabats were dropped on to a SWAPO training camp at Cassinga inside Angola. The target was bombed by the South African Air Force (SAAF) and the paratroops were supposed to sweep through and seize any useful intelligence they could find. To their astonishment, the Parabats found themselves engaged in a desperate battle with over 1,000 heavily-armed guerrillas fighting from well-sited defensive positions. The site was surrounded by 23mm anti-aircraft guns which the guerrillas turned on the paratroops. These were eventually taken out with hand-held 60mm mortars and grenade attacks and the enemy resistance crumbled. However, after about half the force had been airlifted out by helicopter, a column of Cuban tanks and armoured personnel carriers appeared out of the bush to launch a counter-attack. The leading tank struck a mine laid by the Parabats on the approach road and the Cubans halted. The SAAF intervened, some fighter-bombers continuing to swoop low over the enemy even after they had run out of ammunition. The Parabats managed to break contact and were airlifted to safety.

The Cassinga raid inflicted severe casualties on SWAPO, destroyed a large stockpile of weapons and ammunition and provided much important intelligence. It took the guerrillas several years to recover and their training bases were set back even further north.

The growing importance of airborne operations was recognised and in 1978 P.W. Botha, the South African President, announced the creation of 44th Parachute Brigade: an all-arms airborne formation including three parachute battalions; engineers, signals and heavy weapons companies.

Organisation

The 1st Parachute Battalion is now a training unit. The 44th Parachute Brigade includes the 2nd, 3rd and 4th Parachute Battalions plus an anti-tank, a despatch and a path-finder company; the 44th Para Engineer Regiment; 44th Signal Unit; 44th Maintenance Unit; 37th Field Workshop and 7th Medical Group. The 101st Air Supply Company conducts heavy equipment drops and the Brigade has its own anti-aircraft and light artillery regiments. All these units are volunteer regular soldiers, but the Brigade does include one Citizen Force (national service) element: 14th Parachute Battalion Group. This consists of conscripts who have completed one year's training with the 1st Parachute Battalion.

Selection and Training
The training programme for the South African Parachute Brigade is predictably arduous, with tremendous emphasis on physical strength and fitness. It is no longer restricted to white units. The first Zulu volunteers began airborne training in 1990 and their already excellent fitness allowed them to sail through parts of the course that usually defeat a high proportion of entrants.

Weapons and equipment
The United Nations orchestrated an arms embargo against South Africa in the hope that this could bring the Defence Force to its knees. The policy has had exactly the opposite effect: the Republic is now one of the top ten arms exporters in the world! South African paratroopers are armed with the R4 5.56mm assault rifle which has replaced

Below: One "Parabat" in camp, but the presence of five R4 5.56mm assault rifles indicates that others are close at hand.

license-built versions of the 7.62mm FN FAL and G3 rifles. The R4 is a variant of the Israeli Galil rifle which incorporates a number of changes necessary because of the very different operating conditions found in southern Africa. The butt is longer since the average South African soldier is of larger stature than an Israeli. The furniture is reinforced-plastic and the receiver and gas piston are slightly different. The overall result is an even stronger rifle, ideal for the harsh conditions of bush warfare where ready access to maintenance facilities cannot be guaranteed.

Now it has a heavy drop capability, the Brigade is acquiring a variety of air-droppable vehicles including modified Land Rovers and locally-built utility vehicles which increase the mobility of the paratroopers once on the ground.

Uniform
South African Parabats wear the standard khaki combat uniform of the South African Defence Force (see Reconnaissance Commandos). Although British-style webbing remained in service for years, the SADF has been experimenting with an interesting selection of chest-rigs modelled on those worn by the guerrillas. These are ideal for soldiers who want to carry large quantities of ammunition that they can get at quickly.

Reconnaissance Commandos

After over two decades of conflict in southern Africa, the South African Defence Force (SADF) is no longer involved in military operations beyond the borders of the Republic. In 1990 South Africa withdrew from Namibia as part of an agreement with the Soviet Union, Cuba and the SWAPO guerrilla movement. Namibia was granted independence while Cuban forces were withdrawn from Angola. President Gorbachev has ceased to supply military assitance to the communist regime in Angola, thus ending the most serious external threat to South Africa.

The war in Namibia and Angola led the SADF to create a number of special forces units. These include No. 32 Battalion, recruited from Angolan soldiers whose army was defeated by the communists in the civil war, but the unquestioned elite are the Reconnaissance Commandos or "Recces".

The primary Recce mission is to operate deep inside enemy territory, gaining information and tracking enemy units. This is a similar task to that of the erstwhile Selous Scouts of the Rhodesian Army, and it could well be that a number of former members of that outfit have joined South Africa's Reconnaissance Commandos.

All Recce soldiers are trained parachutists, qualifying in both static and free-fall techniques, with many capable of HALO insertion. A number also recieve training in seaborne operations, including underwater swimming. Tracking and survival in the bush are obviously essential, together with the usual special forces skills in using explosives, radios, enemy weapons, and in unarmed combat. They also qualify as paramedics.

Selection and training

Selection courses for the Recce Commandos are of 42 weeks' duration and are held twice a year. Unlike many other such courses they are open not only to volunteers from the South African army, but from the navy and air force as well.

The average age of those attending the course is 19, and only about 6 to 10 per cent are ultimately successful. Medical and psychological tests are necessary preliminaries to attending the selection course, as is the physical test which includes: covering 20 miles (32km) in 6 hours carrying full equipment, R4 rifle and a 70lb (32kg) sand-bag; various physical exercises (e.g. 40 push-ups) within a specified time, and timed runs; swimming free-style for 50 yards (47m).

The selection courses takes place in Zululand, and is carried out in an operational environment. The standards set are extremely tough, and great emphasis is placed on pushing the volunteers to the limit. One of the final tests, for example, is to make the men spend one or two nights alone in the bush, with just a rifle and some ammunition to protect themselves from wild animals. The result of all this is to produce a very highly skilled, capable, and motivated soldier, who is thoroughly at home in the combat environment of today's southern Africa, either on his own or as a member of a group.

Weapons and equipment

The "Recces" use the full spectrum of SADF infantry weapons including the R4 assault rifle and the new SS77 general-purpose machine-gun.

Uniform

Recce Commandos wear standard South African khaki although some were reported as wearing Portuguese-style camouflage used by the Angolan Army during the 1987-88 invasion.

Right: One of South Africa's elite Reconnaissance Commandos on a punitive mission inside enemy territory, departs a burning village that was once a terrorist's haven. Missions of this nature were a regular occurrence when South Africa clashed with guerilla forces operating in Namibia and Angola during the 1970s and 1980s.

Combat hat

Blackened face

Light khaki combat uniform

Green canvas webbing equipment

Combat knife

Ammunition pouches

Water bottle

7.62mm FN FAL rifle

Map pocket

53

Airborne Forces

The Soviet Army was the first to pioneer airborne operations. It formed a parachute unit in 1931 and during exercises in 1935, 2,500 paratroopers conducted an airborne landing, astonishing western observers who had been invited by Stalin. Today, the Soviets field the world's largest airborne forces: seven divisions backed up by air-droppable armoured vehicles and a huge fleet of helicopter gunships.

The airborne forces are part of the Soviet Army but are not directly under its command. They are subordinated directly to the Ministry of Defence and are regarded as a strategic reserve. Recruited mostly from Slav races, they showed no compunction in quelling nationalist disturbances in the Baltic republics and Armenia. This role as protector of the Party is ironic since the founders of the Soviet airborne forces all perished in Stalin's purge of the army just before World War II. The elimination of so many officers effectively destroyed the Red Army's airborne arm, and the paratroop operations between 1941 and 1945 never rivalled those of Germany or the Allies. Those that were attempted were only a small scale and most ended in disaster. The airborne forces were constantly handicapped by a lack of transport aircraft and the Red Army's paratroops were used throughout the war as elite infantry.

During the years of confrontation between NATO and the Warsaw Pact, the airborne forces trained to spearhead the Soviet invasion of West Germany. They were ready ▶

Right: A mass drop of Soviet paratroops. The Soviet Army was the great pioneer of airborne operations and today has the largest parachute force in the world with no less than 7 divisions at full strength.

Below: Soviet paratrooper in his jumping gear. The D-1 parachute on his back is limited to a minimum height of 492ft (150m) and a speed of 189 knots.

'Right: Soviet paratroopers man a twin 23mm ZU-23 anti-aircraft weapon. There are 6 weapons per battery and one battery in each parachute regiment.

▶ to seize key river crossings — such as those over the River Wesser which would have cut 1 (British) Corps in half. It would have been very much like the Allied assault on Arnhem during World War II: airborne forces descending deep behind enemy lines to occupy vital positions and hold them until the advancing ground troops could break through and link up. Whereas most other Soviet land forces emphasise offensive tactics in their exercises, the Soviet paratroops are well-trained in defending their objectives against the inevitable counter-attack. Again in contrast with the rest of the Soviet Army, the airborne divisions also stress close-quarter fighting in built-up areas.

The Soviets are under no illusion that a parachute drop can work against an alert enemy equipped with modern anti-aircraft weapons. Airdrops would rely on surprise, massive supporting fire from aircraft, and missiles or NBC weapons to suppress the defences. Airdrops are normally conducted under cover of darkness and take place as close to the objective as possible. To increase the mobility of their paratroopers once on the ground, the Soviets have developed a range of armoured personnel carriers (APCs) that can be air-dropped into position.

The airborne forces have spearheaded several Soviet military operations in recent years. The 103rd Guards Airborne Division seized Prague airport in 1968 and the 105th Guards Airborne Division led the initial assault on Kabul during

Below: BMD airborne combat vehicle on parade. There are 330 in each airborne division. Infantry versions are armed with a 73mm gun, Sagger ATGW and ▶ **a co-axial 7.62mm machine-gun.**

56

Above: The BMD is designed to be dropped by parachute and provides mobile firepower for Soviet parachute units. It is a well-designed and highly capable fighting vehicle.

Below: Soviet paratroops and aircrew pose for a formal camera shot in front of an Ilyushin Il-76 "Candid" aircraft. Note the blue berets and reserve parachutes worn on the chest.

► the 1979 invasion of Afghanistan. In the Afghan War, the airborne forces proved their worth as idealogically-sound shock troops. Conducting helicopter assaults from Mi-8 "Hips" and Mi-24 "Hinds", the airborne troops were feared by the *Mujahideen* for their ability to mount surprise attacks into guerrilla strongholds.

Organisation

The seven Soviet airborne divisions are Category I (full readiness) although the 106th Guards Airborne at Ryazan is usually employed in a training role. There is also the 44th Guards Airborne Division which is merely a skeleton formation for paratroop training. The airborne forces were re-organised in 1980 when the 105th Guards Airborne Division was disbanded, and its position at Bagram, Afghanistan, was taken over by the 103rd Guards Airborne Division. The latter fought throughout the war and left its BMD armoured fighting vehicles to the Afghan government when President Gorbachev withdrew Soviet forces in the late-1980s.

The strategic mobility of the airborne forces is still restricted by the availability of transport aircraft.

At current estimates of Soviet strength, they have enough aircraft to make a long-range airborne assault with just one division. For a short-range operation they could probably land two or three divisions together. Alternatively, the airborne divisions could go into action without their BMDs and heavy equipment. Of the 600 or so Il-76 "Candid" sorties required to land a division only 40 are needed for the men: landing the BMDs demands over 100 and it takes nearly 450 to deliver the 1,000 + trucks and motor vehicles that are operated by each division. ►

Right: Soviet paratroops deploy from their BMD. Note the leather helmets, one-piece suits and 7.62mm AKM assault rifles. A total of 7 men can be carried, including driver and commander.

Below: ASU-85 air-portable self-propelled anti-tank guns moving off from their Antonov An-12s. The excellent ASU-85 was first seen in 1962 and there is a battalion of 32 with each airborne division. Weapons are one 85mm anti-tank gun, one 7.62mm MG and one 12.7mm AAMG.

Above: A stick of Soviet paratroops during a winter exercise. These elite men are well-trained and enthusiastic, but suffer from the problems of a conscript army.

Above right: Paratrooper (note badge on right sleeve) carrying 5.45mm AK-74S assault rifle. The working parts of the rifle can be seen, especially the muzzle brake and leaf backsight.

▶ In addition to the airborne divisions proper, there are a number of airmobile (heliborne) assault battalions attached to Armies and several air assault brigades. The latter are paratroop trained and partially equipped with BMDs, but they have no helicopters: they would rely on Soviet Frontal Aviation to provide them for specific operations. These brigades are about 2,500-strong, while the airborne divisions consist of over 6,500 men organised into:
3 airborne regiments (c.1,500 men in 3 battalions)
1 air defence battalion (SA-7 missiles and ZU-23 AA guns)
1 artillery regiment (D-30 122mm howitzers)
1 engineer battalion
1 signals battalion
1 reconnaissance company
1 NBC defence company
1 transport battalion
1 maintenance battalion
1 medical battalion
Although few women serve in frontline Soviet units, some female

Right: With the demise of the Communist state, the sight of a political officer explaining the contents of Pravda to a group of Airborne paratroopers is all but a thing of the past.

medics were on active service with the airborne forces in Afghanistan.

Selection and training
While tank and motor rifle divisions always contain a significant proportion of raw recruits at any one time, the airborne forces receive the best of each year's conscripts. Like the Strategic Rocket Forces, the airborne divisions receive soldiers who have already undergone some training and many will have already learned to parachute in the DOSAAF paramilitary youth organisation. Soviet airborne training is extremely tough, even by Soviet Army standards. The airborne divisions contain a much higher proportion of professional soldiers and long-service NCOs than other units in the Soviet Army. ▶

▶ Weapons and equipment

Individual paratroopers are armed with the outstanding AK-74S 5.45mm assault rifle. This has a folding stock and can be distinguished from early versions of the Kalashnikov by a prominent groove along the foregrip and its distinctive muzzle-brake. The latter is a superb feat of engineering and funnels much of the blast sideways — a great aid to accurate rapid fire. The AK-74 has very light recoil and is capable of great accuracy. Some were seen in Afghanistan fitted with telescopic sights.

Each division is equipped with over 300 BMD APCs. These air-droppable vehicles can carry up to six paratroops in their tiny troop compartment and are armed with

Above: Heliborne assaults and gunship support missions are conducted by Mil M-24 "Hinds".

AT-4 "Spigot" anti-tank missiles, three 7.62mm machine-guns and either a 30mm cannon or the smooth-bore 73mm gun. They are fully amphibious even without preparation. A support version, NATO designation SO-120, carries a breech-loading 120mm mortar.

The Soviet paratroop battalions include a very high proportion of light machine-guns — 5.56mm RPK-74s — and light anti-tank

Below: As one paratrooper lands, some of his comrades press forward supported by an air-droppable BMD APC.

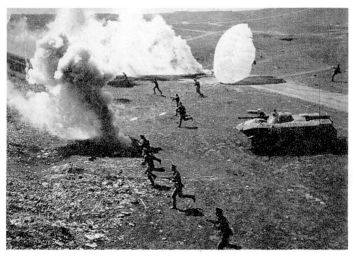

weapons — RPG-16s, RPG-18s and SPG-9s. For air defence, the paratroops rely on 23mm ZU-23 twin anti-aircraft guns and SA-7 anti-aircraft missiles.

Uniform

The Soviet Army has recently introduced a mottled camouflage uniform in dark green and khaki, but the old "computer pattern" camouflage was still being used after the end of the Afghan War. The airborne forces wear blue berets, usually seen set at a jaunty angle well back on the head. Their disctinctive striped shirt is that traditionally worn by the naval units fighting for the Bolsheviks during the revolution. It was adopted by the airborne forces during the 1950s when they were modernised by a former commander of Naval

Above: As with so many of the world's elite forces, the training for Airborne Forces is both tough and realistic. Armed with 5.54mm AKR sub machine-gun, the lead trooper provides cover for a group of officer cadets after taking a bridge.

Infantry, Major-General V.F. Margelov. Blue collar tabs and shoulder-boards are also worn, displaying the insignia of the airborne forces. In combat the Soviet paratroops wear peaked caps camouflaged in the same pattern as the new smock and trousers. Subdued insignia were developed during the war in Afghanistan. There, the paratroops wore the floppy "bush" hat or khaki cap sported by most Soviet units fighting the *Mujahideen*.

Naval Infantry

The Naval Infantry is one of the Soviet Union's smallest military formations. No more than 20,000 strong, it is divided between the Soviet Navy's four fleets: two regiments deployed with the Northern Fleet, one each with the Black Sea and Baltic Fleets, and a brigade with the Pacific Fleet. Less than one-tenth of the size of the US Marine Corps, the Naval Infantry is not intended for the sort of strategic role undertaken by the Marines in World War II, Korea, Vietnam and Operation *Desert Storm*. Rather, it is intended to seize key points in advance of an amphibious invasion and to attack behind enemy lines. During World War II, the Naval Infantry mounted over 100 landings, but only four involved more than 2,000 troops: the rest were platoon or company-sized raids. Until recently, the Naval Infantry lacked the capability to do very much more than this, but as new weapons and equipment are adopted, the strategic potential of the Naval Infantry is certainly increasing.

Naval Infantry have had a checkered career in the history of the Soviet Union. Originally founded by Tsar Peter the Great, they were disbanded by Alexander I after the Napoleonic Wars. Naval Infantry units were raised for the Crimean War and Russo-Japanese War, but it was not until the Russian Revolution that they became a significant force. However, after the Civil War was over, they were abolished. During World War II the Soviet Union ultimately fielded 350,000 Naval Infantry, organised into 40 brigades, six independent regiments and several small units. The reason was simple: the Navy had never really recovered from the revolution and it could accomplish little against the Germans. The Fleet was drained of manpower to fight in the critical land battles that decided World War II. Few of these brigades had any amphibious training or equipment — they were simply infantrymen in a different uniform. In 1947 the complete ▶

Right: Unarmed, hand-to-hand combat has to be learnt by all Naval Infantry recruits for close-quarter confrontations.

Below: Soviet Naval Infantry PT-76 Model 2 being unloaded from an Aist class air-cushion vehicle on a training exercise.

▶ organisation was disbanded.

Naval Infantry were re-established in 1961 and appropriate amphibious warfare ships were constructed to give each of the fleets a limited landing capability.

Organisation

Each regiment consists of three motor rifle battalions and a fourth which is airborne-trained but not provided with its own air transport. This is intended to be landed by the fleet's helicopters, aircraft from Frontal Aviation or hovercraft. In 1988 the Soviet Union announced that it was re-assigning two motor rifle divisions to the Northern Fleet for coastal defence. This was simply an easy means of evading the Conventional Forces in Europe treaty which limited the number of *army* divisions NATO and the Soviet Union could deploy in Europe. There is no evidence that these army units have actually been integrated with the Naval Infantry.

Below: Soviet Naval Infantry undergo very rigorous training and are expected to be equally at home on the land and at sea.

A Naval Infantry regiment consists of three or four battalions of infantry equipped with BTR series 8 x 8 armoured personnel carriers (APCs), and an armoured battalion of 31 main battle tanks (MBTs) and at least 10 amphibious light tanks. Reconnaissance is conducted by one company with BRDM armoured cars, four ZSU-23-4 anti-aircraft guns and four BRDM-2s with SA-9 surface-to-air missiles. They are supported by a battery of BM-21 122mm multiple rocket launchers and have engineer, signal, air defence, chemical defence, transport, supply, maintenance and medical companies.

Selection and training

The Naval Infantry are conscripts but include a higher proportion of career soldiers and NCOs than regular motor rifle divisions. They include many more parachute-trained personnel and battalions trained in helicopter operations.

Weapons and equipment

The Naval Infantry use the standard range of Soviet Infantry weapons and their armoured vehicles are not

of the latest type. They continued
using BTR-60PB wheeled APCs long
after many motor rifle battalions had
converted to BMPs. The BTR-60 has
been modernised — there are now
BTR-70s and -80s but they are still
lightly armoured 8 x 8 APCs with
very poor amphibious performance.
The Naval Infantry's tank battalions ▶

Above: Polnocny class LSTs of
the Soviet Navy unloading BTR
60PB APCs and a single PT-76
reconnaissance tank.

Below: Black uniform, striped
T-shirt and anchor device on
helmet and sleeve clearly identify
the the Soviet Naval infantry.

Above: The black uniform and blue-and-white striped shirt are clearly shown in this view of six Naval Infantry. Their relaxed demeanour is offset by their clearly-visible AK-47s.

▶ retained obsolete T-55 MBTs into the 1980s although they are now obtaining T-72s Those battalions that retained the T-55 may have done so because up to one-third of them were actually TO-55 flamethrower tanks.

The standard Soviet amphibious light tank is the PT-76; a large but poorly-protected vehicle with an inadequate 76mm gun as its main armament. On the other hand, it is mechanically reliable with an excellent cross-country performance and the Soviets have always believed that a small force in the right place at the right time is preferable to a large force arriving too late. There are no signs of a replacement for the PT-76, perhaps because of the increased reliance on hovercraft to ferry men and vehicles to the beach rather than "swimming" ashore in amphibians.

The Soviet Navy is unique in its operation of massive hovercraft —

particularly the Aist class that can carry two MBTs, or 3 BTR APCs and 100 infantrymen, or 60 tons of stores. Travelling at 80 knots, they can deliver troops with great rapidity. The smaller Gus, Lebed and Utenok classes complement these amphibous leviathans and work with the Ivan Rogov class Landing Ship Tanks that came into service during the 1980s. These vessels include a helicopter deck and a well dock capable of taking three Gus hovercraft; they can carry and land an entire battalion of Naval Infantry. They have been used to take the Naval Infantry away from their traditional landing sites in the Baltic and to carry out amphibious exercises in far-off Syria.

Uniform

The Naval Infantry still wear the blue and white striped shirt made famous by their Bolshevik predecessors (see Soviet Airborne Forces) and a black uniform. The latter is patterned like the army's olive drab field service uniform. Depending on the terrain and time of year, the Naval Infantry wear the "computer pattern" camouflage smocks that became universal in the Soviet ground forces during the 1980s. Made of a coarse material in numerous shades of green, these have a random pattern of rectangular grey areas and can be worn over or under a soldier's personal equipment. The Naval Infantry continue a tradition of painting the outline of a red star on their SSh-60 steel helmets which also sport an anchor insignia on the side. However, these distinctions are often concealed beneath a camouflage cover.

Below: A riverine operation by Soviet Naval Infantry. This force is regarded by many as one of the Soviet elites and has "Guards" status, which is not granted lightly within the Soviet armed forces.

Spetsnaz

Spetsnaz is an abbreviation of *voiska spetsialnoye naznacheniya*, which means "special designation troops". It is a term used in the Soviet Union to describe western special forces such as the Special Air Service or the US *Delta Force*. During the 1980s the name was applied by western analysts to certain elite units of the Soviet armed forces. This has created the impression that Spetsnaz is a single organisation comparable to the US Special Operations Command. However, there is no evidence that this is the case; just as the Soviet Union relies on two organisations for internal security — the KGB (Committee for State Security) and the MVD (Ministry of Internal Security) — several different elements of the Soviet military machine have established their own elite formations.

The use of small elite units dates back to the foundation of the Communist state itself. The Red Army used special forces-type units during the Russian Civil War and the Cheka — forerunner of the KGB — used special detachments to spearhead the campaign against muslim rebels in Central Asia during the 1920s. During World War II special army units were landed behind the German lines to organise partisan resistance and to attack important targets such as rail centres. When the Soviet Union launched its surprise attack on Japan in 1945, special engineer detachments parachuted into the mountains to secure vital tunnels that the Soviets needed for their invasion of Manchuria. Other special forces units were landed on South Sakhalin and the Kurile Islands.

The special warfare units called Spetsnaz in the West certainly spearheaded the Soviet invasion of Czechoslovakia in 1968. Plain-clothed soldiers under the control of the GRU (Military Intelligence Directorate) occupied Prague airport to allow the bloodless landing of the 103rd Guards Airborne Division. The intervention in Afghanistan began in the same way in 1979, although with less success. On 27 December of that year, Soviet troops seized control of key government buildings and communications facilities in the Afghan capital, Kabul. The 105th Guards Airborne Division, which had landed at Bagram 12 miles (19km) away on 24 December began to advance on Kabul. Reports of what happened next are fragmentary but it seems that a KGB assault team tried and failed to kill the Afghan President in the Darulamin Palace. President Amin rallied some loyal troops and a handful of T-55 tanks and was only ▶

Right: A Spetsnaz soldier with an SA-7 "Grail" man-portable missile launcher. Operations would be conducted from deep within enemy territory.

Below: One of the essentials for Spetsnaz soldiers is a very high level of physical fitness.

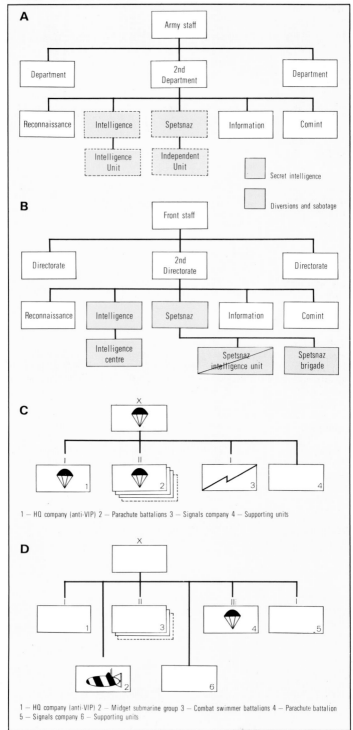

1 — HQ company (anti-VIP) 2 — Parachute battalions 3 — Signals company 4 — Supporting units

1 — HQ company (anti-VIP) 2 — Midget submarine group 3 — Combat swimmer battalions 4 — Parachute battalion
5 — Signals company 6 — Supporting units

Information derived from a Viktor Suvorov article in International Defense Review

overrun after a sharp battle which cost the Soviet airborne forces several of their armoured vehicles. Amin, his family, advisors and palace guards were all slain. Two of the Soviets' special forces commanders were killed in action: Colonel U. Bayerenov, commander of the KGB special operations school at Balishika and Major-General V.S. Paputin of the MVD.

Organisation

The GRU works in parallel with the KGB and operates spy networks all over the world. According to a GRU defector who writes under the pseudonym Viktor Suvorov, it also includes 16 brigades of special operations troops which are controlled not by the appropriate army headquarters, but directly from the GRU itself. These GRU soldiers are in three types of unit:

● *Razvedchiki* ("Scouts")
Each Soviet army division has a reconnaissance battalion, one company of which specialises in long-range recce patrols. Each Army-level headquarters has such a company as well and these are airborne-qualified. These recce specialists are comparable to the US Army's LRRP companies.

● *Raydoviki* ("Raiders")
Independent battalions comparable to the US Army Ranger battalions. Airborne-qualified, they fight in companies or battalions rather than small patrols and are trained as elite shock troops.

● *Vysotniki* ("Rangers")
More comparable to the British SAS, these troops work in small units on long-range missions far behind enemy lines.

There are also four naval Spetsnaz brigades, one attached to each fleet. These include three battalions of combat swimmers plus an airborne battalion. There are other specialists in the formation including midget submarines. These naval forces are trained to pave the way for an amphibious assault in the same way as the British SBS or US Navy SEALs. They are also ready to attack harbour installations and other coastal facilities. Reports persist that they operate in Swedish waters, monitoring Swedish defences and planting surveillance devices.

In addition to these military units, any assessment of Soviet special forces should include the KGB Special Troops. The borderline between spies, agents and soldiers becomes very blurred here and the KGB — whatever its commitment to *glasnost* over the last few years ▶

Left: Spetsnaz control organisation at Army (A) and Front/Fleet (B) levels. Peacetime organisation is into army brigades (C) and naval brigades (D). In war Spetsnaz would fight in small groups coming together into larger groups for specific operations.

Below: Spetsnaz paratroopers participate in a Soviet Army assault exercise. The rifle being aimed is a 5.54mm AKS-74U with a folding butt and a 30-round plastic magazine.

▶ — has never revealed full details of its organisation. The KGB is known internationally for espionage but its main business is the Border Guards Directorate — a paramilitary force over 300,000-strong that includes armoured vehicles and naval units. The Border Guards are elite by Soviet definition because they are chosen from the most politically reliable citizens. Used in the frontline during World War II, they also fought in Afghanistan during the 1980s. The increase in aircraft hijackings on Aeroflot (the state airline) has led the KGB to form a hostage rescue unit which was first reported by *Red Star* in March 1989. This followed several botched operations by MVD special units that resulted in hostages being killed. The KGB has encroached on to traditional MVD territory here but its hostage rescue team, based at KGB headquarters in Dzershinsky Square has seen further action and begun to establish contacts abroad. In 1991 a deputation visited the SAS in the UK to study British counter-terrorist tactics.

Below: For many years, the primary target for Spetsnaz operations was to have been NATO forces and bases. To enhance training, accurate mock-ups of NATO equipment (especially that with a nuclear role) were built.

Selection and training

While the KGB and GRU undoubtedly maintain a few small bodies of professionals for the most sensitive tasks, the overwhelming majority of the units described as Spetsnaz are conscripts, drafted for two years in the case of the army, or three for the navy. While operations in Afghanistan showed them to be extremely tough soldiers, there has been a tendency in the West to exaggerate their capabilities — crediting the Soviet Union with training 20,000 men to the standards of the SAS or *Delta Force*.

The majority of Spetsnaz forces are certainly elite formations, but their status is at least partly derived from the generally low standard of the average motor rifle division. Soviet army commanders were disagreeably surprised in Afghanistan, where combat experience showed the ordinary conscript infantry to be poorly trained and equipped to deal with the guerrillas. This has led to a wholesale revision of equipment and tactics which is beginning to take effect, but it meant that the burden of the war against the *mujahideen* fell largely on specialist troops. All major offensives in Afghanistan were mounted by airborne units, divisional reconnaissance battalions, helicopter assault battalions or other elite light infantry. Ordinary motor rifle units were left to guard key points. ▶

Above: Spetsnaz troops must, of course, be extremely fit and the USSR also fields excellent sports teams in world events. In fact, they combine the two requirements and there are many cases of athletes later being identified as members of covert units.

Below: India class submarines act as "mother-ships" for the tracked mini-subs operated by naval Spetsnaz units. Since the early-1980s, mini-subs have conducted operations in Swedish territorial waters in preparation for another war.

▶ The personnel selected for Spetsnaz units are like those ear-marked for the airborne divisions: politically reliable, extremely strong and fit and probably part parachute-trained thanks to experience in DOSAAF. Yet even if a potential recruit excelled in all these characteristics and had the intelligence and aptitude for independent operations behind enemy lines, his two years' military service do not leave much time to employ him after his training is complete. Western elite units understand that it takes many months to achieve their exacting standards, and if other key skills are added to the list — foreign languages, cross-training in demolitions, medical techniques and communications systems — it is obvious why western special warfare units recruit from volunteer soldiers who already have some military experience.

Weapons and equipment

Spetsnaz forces fighting in Afghanistan made use of several new weapons not encountered in the hands of ordinary infantry battalions. Silenced weapons were used — both the 1950s-vintage silenced Stechkin machine-pistol and a clip-on suppressor for the 7.62mm AKM rifle. Spetsnaz units were among the first to employ the AK-74 5.45mm assault rifle and then the AKS-74U — a shortened version the size of a sub-machine gun, fitted with a collapsible stock for good measure. They wore body armour and used scopes on their AKs as well as night vision equipment, and by the mid-1980s some units were using a single-shot grenade launcher. This fits under the barrel of a Kalashnikov rather like the American M203 under an M16. Several exotic weapons appeared as well, including the spring-loaded knife that shoots its blade across a room and the sharpened entrenching tool which can be thrown like an axe.

Uniform

Spetsnaz have no uniform to distinguish them from airborne or naval forces; indeed, in Afghanistan they sometimes wore the uniform of the Afghan army, or even dressed as tribesmen. Normally they wore the sort of combat smocks issued to the Airborne Divisions and the KGB Border Guards.

Below: To be able to parachute behind enemy lines is a key aspect of Spetsnaz training and operational doctrine. In this view, parachute-equipped troops make their way into a Mil Mi-8 "Hip" helicopter at the beginning of yet another in a long line of realistic air-drop training sorties undertaken by Spetsnaz forces.

Right: Alert to any movement, a Spetsnaz soldier carefully makes his way through what remains of an enemy outpost. He is armed with an AKS-74 sub-machine gun, complete with tubular skeleton butt that folds by swinging to the left and lying alongside the SMG's receiver. A bayonet can also be fitted.

Long Range Amphibious Reconnaissance Commandos

When Chiang Kai-shek and the last of the Nationalist Chinese forces were compelled to leave mainland China on December 7, 1949, they swore that one day they would return. Today, 35 years later, that remains their stated aim despite the immense power of the Communist mainland and virtual abandonment by the USA. So great is this determination that the government even issues two annual budgets: one "provincial" budget for Taiwan, and a second "national" budget for the mainland.

The Army is very efficient and well-trained, and is currently some 330,000 strong. Their deployment is split between the main island of Taiwan, some 100 miles (160km) offshore, and the two inshore islands of Quemoy and Matsu, both of which are within artillery range of the mainland. The Quemoy garrison is some 60,000 strong and that of Matsu some 20,000. There have been several crises over this situation, particularly in 1954, 1955 and 1957 but, although there have been no overwhelming threats of late, the potential for trouble remains. The government on Taiwan maintains very large armed forces, which are very efficient and highly trained, but are also a substantial drain on the economy.

Included in Taiwan's army are four special forces groups, which include the Long-range Amphibious Reconnaissance Commandos, and para-frogmen. There are also two brigades of paratroopers. The Recce Commandos are very highly trained and are known to have been active on the mainland in the maritime provinces for many years.

There is a growing relationship, including between special forces, between the four isolated countries of Israel, South Africa, Singapore and Taiwan. Advisers are exchanged, weapons bought and sold, are "know-how" passed from one to another.

Weapons and equipment

Standard rifle of the Taiwan Army is the M16A1, of which some 5,000 have been supplied direct from the USA. The Combined Services Arsenal at Kaohsuing has, however, produced a new rifle — designated the 5.56mm Type 65 — which is now in service with Taiwan special forces, including the Long-Range Amphibious Reconnaissance Commandos. This bears some similarities to the M16A1, although it also has features taken from the AR-18 design.

The standard sub-machine gun is the 0.45 Type 36, a locally produced version of the US M3A1. Standard light machine-gun is the US M60 7.62mm, made under licence in Taiwan. Obtaining weapons is becoming a major problem as the PRC imposes pressure on former suppliers.

Uniform

Up till now the uniform of the Taiwanese forces has been almost totally American in design and appearance, although this influence may diminish as the USA seeks closer ties with the People's Republic and distances itself more and more from its former allies on Taiwan.

Right: Soldier of Taiwan's elite Long-Range Recce Commandos demonstrates his martial arts prowess. Western forces are at last starting to appreciate the value of such skills and are teaching them to their special forces. Not only do such martial arts train men in unarmed combat techniques, but they also improve physical fitness and mental discipline. Taiwan's commandos have much combat experience and have been active on the offshore islands, and probably on the mainland as well, since the Kuomintang forces were expelled from the mainland in December 1949.

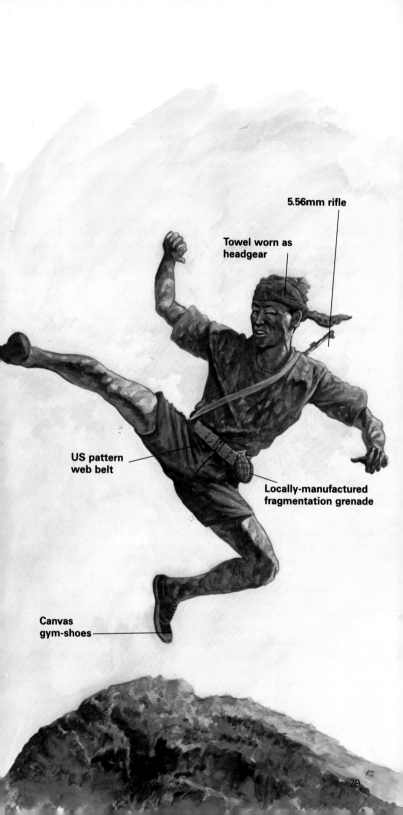

5.56mm rifle

Towel worn as
headgear

US pattern
web belt

Locally-manufactured
fragmentation grenade

Canvas
gym-shoes

79

Army Special Forces

Thailand has long had both external and internal defence problems. The Communist insurgents in Malaysia have used southern Thailand as a sanctuary for many years, and they have had repeated clashes with the Thai military forces. There are also tensions on the border with Burma, but the biggest problems are on the eastern border with Kampuchea, where the Royal Thai Army finds itself face-to-face with the Vietnamese Army, the most experienced land force in Asia.

The Royal Thai Army had an airborne Ranger battalion for some years and in 1963 this was re-organised and redesignated 1st Special Forces Group (Airborne); since then 2nd, 3rd and 4th Special Forces Groups have been raised, and were recently redsignated regiments. Their tasks include unconventional warfare behind the enemy lines, psychological operations, civic actions and, above all, counter-insurgency. One of the principal activities in the counter-insurgency field is the organisation, training and equipping of village defence units to look after village defence and also to provide support for army (and especially, of course, Special Forces) operations in their respective areas.

Organisation

In 1984 the Thai army created the Special Warfare Command to co-ordinate its various elite units. This is also known as No. 5 Army Region, making its commander a lieutenant-general equal to the officers commanding the four military regions. There are now five regiments, organised into two divisions: No. 1 Division (Nos. 1, 2, and 3 Regiments) is based at Camp

Above: A Thai Special Forces trooper secures his parachute.

Above: Training in the martial arts is based on Thai boxing.

Erawan together with the Long Range Reconnaissance Company, the Airborne Resupply Battalion and the Psyops Battalion. No. 2 Division (Nos. 4 and 5 Regiments) is at Phitsanulok and Chieng Mai.

Selection and training
Volunteers for the Special Forces must first complete both parachute and Ranger schools before admission to the Special Forces regiments, where they undergo further training. There is also a survival centre, where the many specialised skills of jungle survival are taught.

Great attention is paid to physical fitness, especially to a form of martial arts based upon traditional Thai boxing, a highly effective activity which involves the use not

Left: Thai Special Forces soldier in the jungle which covers a large part of the country. Tough and determined fighters, the Thai soldiers have been battling with guerillas and the Vietnamese Army for many years.

only of the hands, but of feet as well. There is also emphasis on parachute training.

Weapons and equipment
The Army Special Forces use the M-17A1 rifle and the shortened version, the CAR-15. Like the Thai Marine Recon, they use the H&K MP5 9mm sub-machine-gun and also the 7.62mm G-3 and 5.56mm HK 33 which are both manufactured under license in Thailand.

Uniform
The main symbol of the Special Forces is a red beret with a gold woven national army cap badge. Working uniform is a two-piece camouflage suit, with low-visibility black embroidered rank and qualification badges. The same uniform is worn on operations, but with a camouflaged "jungle hat". A special combat uniform is also sometimes used, comprising a black suit and black boots, topped with a black knitted balaclava helmet; an outfit obviously modelled on that used by the British SAS.

Gurkhas

It was widely expected that the British Government's 1991 defence cuts would spell the end of a unique military unit, the Gurkhas. Battalions of Nepalese soldiers have served the British forces since 1815, fighting on the North-West frontier of India and ultimately providing over 250,000 men in each World War. It is a strange alliance that has endured the British withdrawal from India and the succession of post-1945 reductions in the British Army. Although the *Options for Change* review will reduce the current five battalions of Gurkhas to two, it seems that few politicians are ready to sever such an enduring and close relationship.

When the United Kingdom granted independence to India, half the Gurkha regiments were alloted to the new Indian army and half remained with the British. Fortunately for their future, British forces were soon embroiled in several Asian wars. The Gurkhas played a distinguished role in the Malayan Emergency and were equally prominent in the "confrontation" with Indonesia. In both conflicts, the Gurkhas proved themselves masters of jungle warfare and worthy successors to the Gurkhas who had fought so hard in Burma during World War II.

The Gurkhas have remained in the Far East, in Hong Kong and Brunei. It has become customary to station a single battalion in the UK but, although Gurkhas have exercised in Germany and even Northern Ireland in the early-1960s, the Army has never integrated them with BAOR. Neither have they been deployed to Ulster since the beginning of "The Troubles" — although there is a school of thought that they might be just the answer.

The last operational deployment of the Gurkhas came during the Falklands campaign when 1/7th Gurkha Rifles went to war as part of 5 Infantry Brigade. To their bitter disappointment, the Argentines surrendered within hours of a planned Gurkha attack on the hills

Below: Led by one of the few British officers within the Gurkha regiments, a patrol slowly makes its way through an urban training area in Hong Kong.

overlooking Port Stanley.

There remains an inevitable question mark over the Gurkhas' long-term future as part of the British Army. Some observers certainly regard them as an anachronism, but those with longer memories still cherish this unique alliance. In times of the gravest danger, no nation has ever proved a more staunch ally of the UK than the mountain kingdom of Nepal. No foreign soldiers have ever fought so hard for the British Army.

Selection and training

The kingdom of Nepal has a surplus of volunteers for the British Gurkha regiments and recruiters are spoiled for choice. Those who are accepted are currently trained in Hong Kong, but this facility will obviously have to be moved before the Chinese take over in 1997. Gurkhas enlist

Above: Gurkha operations deep in the jungle often entail the use of helicopters as a means of entry and exit.

at 17½ years-of-age and serve a minimum of five years.

Uniform and equipment

The Gurkhas wear standard British DPM combat uniforms and are equipped like any other battalion. However, there is ·one famous additional weapon, the *kukri*. This is the Gurkhas' distinctive curved fighting knife about which more tall tales have been told than about any other weapon. The Germans, Japanese and Argentinians all told horror stories about Gurkhas and their *kukris* — stories that the Gurkhas have never denied since it all adds to their ferocious reputation.

Parachute Regiment

The very name of the Parachute Regiment (the "paras") has come to signify both a type of soldiering and a certain "style"—dramatic, forceful and with panache. Paratroops would, it seems, always need to be fighting against heavy odds and either succeed brilliantly or suffer glorious defeats: the one performance that is never allowed is an indifferent one.

Inevitably it was Winston Churchill who demanded that a slightly reluctant War Office should establish a corps of parachutists on the German model and after a somewhat hesitant start the first unit was formed in late 1940. A trial operation against an aqueduct in Italy in February 1941 ended up with little damage to the objective and all the men captured. However, lessons were learned and progress was made.

The 6th Airborne Division landed on the Allied left flank on D-Day June 6, 1944, and successfully accomplished all its tasks, although it suffered when left in the line for some two months as a conventional infantry unit. That episode over, the paras were withdrawn to England and their next employment was at Arnhem where 1st Airborne Division performed with the most exemplary courage, but were in the end overcome, their reputation made for all time. 6th Airborne Division then took part in the Rhine crossings, which went very well.

When World War II ended the paratroops found themselves involved in two activities which have kept them very busy up to the present day. The first has been to fight their country's many small wars in numerous campaigns on virtually every continent. These conflicts have taken the paras to Malaya, Borneo, Palestine, Suez, Aden, Cyprus, Kuwait, North Borneo and Northern Ireland and the Falkland Islands. Their second major post-war campaign has been one of stubborn resistance to the War Office and the Ministry of Defence in its efforts to dispose of the Parachute Regiment altogether.

Right: Corporal of The Parachute Regiment on patrol in Northern Ireland. He is wearing a "flak" vest and carrying a 7.62mm L1A1 Self-Loading Rifle (SLR).

Below: Parachute Regiment anti-tank team wearing the famous, but now outmoded, paratroops helmets and "Dennison" camouflage smocks.

There was a major reduction in parachute troops in the immediate post-war years, and again in the 1960s and 1970s. 16th Parachute Brigade existed in Aldershot from 1949 to 1977 when it was redesignated 6 Field Force in one of the British Army's endless series of reorganisations and only one battalion of the Parachute Regiment was left in the parachute role, with the two other battalions serving elsewhere in the "straight" infantry role. On 1 January 1982 6th Field Force became 5 Infantry Brigade and included among its units 2nd and 3rd Battalions The Parachute Regiment.

When the South Atlantic War blew up suddenly in 1982 these two battalions were hived off to 3 Commando Brigade and sent south with the Marines. In the Falklands these two units performed very well, and at Goose Green 550 men of 2 Para took on 1,400 Argentines and defeated them utterly, even though their commanding officer,

Lt. Col. "H" Jones, died in the battle. In the finest para tradition he died at the head of his men, personally leading an attack against a machine-gun position that was holding up the entire attack. He was posthumously awarded the Victoria Cross.

The paras' methods are nothing if not direct and this has, on several occasions, made them controversial. They have always been among the more successful units in Northern Ireland and thus naturally a target for hostile propaganda. This reached a nadir on January 30, 1972, in the so-called "Bloody Sunday" episode when a crowd of civilians attacked the paras and in the ensuing action some 13 civilians were killed. There was an enormous outcry, but despite this the battalions of the Parachute Regiment have continued to return to Northern Ireland.

In December 1982 the British Secretary of State for Defence, Michael Heseltine, went to Alder- ▶

▶ shot to announce in person that 5 Infantry Brigade was to be redesignated 5 Airborne Brigade.

Organisation

There are three regular battalions: 2 and 3 Para plus three Territorial Army (TA) battalions, 4, 10 and 15 Para. At any one time, two of the regular battalions are assigned to 5 Airborne Brigade which has a full range of supporting units — light artillery, engineers and recce vehicles — which are airborne trained. The brigade has a company of Pathfinders who are trained to land covertly in advance of the main force to prepare the landing sites. Once the brigade has arrived, they are tasked with long-range reconnaissance. The TA battalions were tasked with defending built-up areas in northern Germany if it came to war with the Warsaw Pact, but their role now is rather uncertain.

Selection and training

Would-be paratroops undergo a very arduous training programme cumulating in 'P' Company: a harsh regime that tests recruits endurance, nerve and sense of humour to the very limit. In recent years the regular battalions have remained severely understrength partly because not enough recruits pass out of basic training. The system produces some superb soldiers, but it may have to change if the regiment is to continue at its current strength.

Weapons and equipment

The Parachute Regiment is now equipped with the SA80 5.56mm rifle and the 5.56mm Individual Support Weapon. Like the rest of the British Army, the Regiment has found the new weapons to be superbly accurate on a firing range but rather fragile in the field. The SA80 cannot withstand frequent parachuting so the soldiers will only jump with their weapons if they go into action in wartime. The optical sight, fitted as standard, has been removed by the Pathfinders and other units of 5 Airborne which found it hampered close-range instinctive shooting. Because they may have to face enemy armour without tank support, the battalions have a higher allotment of MILAN anti-tank missiles than other infantry formations. Each battalion has its own mortar platoon equipped with 81mm mortars.

Uniforms

The British paratroops' red beret has been adopted around the world and has given rise to their nicknames of "The Red Devils" and "The Red Berets". (History has it that Major-General Browning and another

---

Wireless Ridge June 13-14, 1982

The battalion attack by 2nd Battalion, The Parachute Regiment (2 Para) on Wireless Ridge, on June 13-14 during the Falklands War in 1982, is an excellent example of an action by a highly trained, fit and experienced infantry unit. This action is of particular interest because 2 Para were the only battalion in the Falklands War to carry out two battalion attacks, and thus the only one to be able to put into practice the lessons learned, in their case at such high cost at Goose Green on May 28.

On June 11, 2 Para was moved by helicopter from Fitzroy on the south coast to a lying-up position west of Mount Kent. At 2300 hours the battalion set off on foot to an assembly area on a hill to the North of Mount Kent, ready to support either 3 Para in their attack on Mount Longdon or 45 Commando Royal Marines, whose mission was to take the position known as Two Sisters. Both these attacks were successful, leaving 3 Para, 45 Commando and 42 Commando firmly established. On June 12, 2 Para moved forward some 9 miles (15km), skirting Mount Longdon on its north-western side, to an assembly area in the lee of a ▶

Right: En route to war, and in a strange environment, British paratroops man machine-guns on board a ship in the South Atlantic in 1982.

general were arguing over the colour of a beret for the paratroops sometime in 1942 and, being unable to agree, they turned to the nearest soldier and asked for his views. "Red, sir," came the instant answer.) The red beret can be worn only by members of the Parachute Regiment (throughout their service) and by members of other Corps who are parachute-qualified, but

Above: British paratrooper on a landing zone with another just landed right behind him. Full effectiveness requires constant, hard and realistic training.

only when on service with a parachute unit. The sleeve badge of the winged Pegasus was designed by Edward Seago, a famous artist.

▶ steep escarpment which offered some cover from the sporadic shelling by the respected Argentine artillery. The battalion, as always, dug-in; orders were received in mid-afternoon for an attack on Wireless Ridge that night, but this was later postponed to the following night.

On June 13 Skyhawk attack aircraft flew in low from the West. Intense fire from the ground prevented the attack from being pressed home, but a number of moves in preparation for the forthcoming battalion action were delayed, especially the registration of targets by the artillery and mortars. At Goose Green 2 Para had been very short of fire support, but in this battle they were to have two batteries of 105mm light guns in direct support, the mortars of both 2 and 3 Para, naval gunfire support from ships within range, as well as the battalion's own machine-gun and MILAN anti-tank missile platoons. Last, but by no means least, a troop of two Scimitar (1 x 30mm cannon) and two Scorpion (1 x 76mm gun) light tanks of The Blues and Royals were an integral part of 2 Para's battle plan.

The battalion moved out at last light (2030 hours local). As they moved to the Forming-Up Places (FUPs), where the troops shake out into battle formations, the sort of report a commanding officer dreads was received: that Intelligence had just discovered a minefield in front of A and B Companies' objective. At this stage, however, there was no alternative but to go ahead.

Right: The Battle of Wireless Ridge took place on June 13/14, 1982, during the South Atlantic War. It was a highly successful battalion attack, incorporating the lessons learned earlier in the brief land campaign. D Company (D) started by taking the Western end of the ridge, following which A Company (A) and B Company (B) took the main position. C Company (C) provided flank protection to the east. Fire support came from tanks, artillery and ships.

The artillery supporting fire started at 0015 hours on June 14 and D Company crossed the start-line at 0045 hours. D Company reached its first objective with little trouble, finding that the enemy had withdrawn, leaving a few dead in their slit trenches. While D Company reorganised, enemy 155mm airburst fire began to fall on their position, a reminder of the efficiency and quick reactions of the Argentine artillery. Meanwhile, A and B Companies began their advance, B Company through what transpired to be the minefield recently discovered by Intelligence.

Some sporadic fire came from a few trenches, but was quickly silenced, and 17 prisoners were taken and a number killed in this ▶

Right: Machine-gunners of the Parachute Regiment training on-board ship. Their weapon is the 7.62mm L7A2 (GPMG).

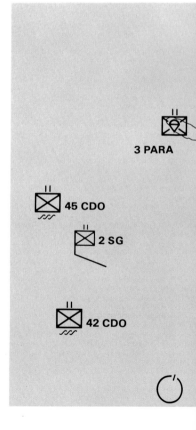

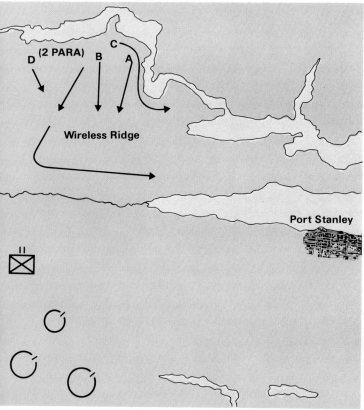

phase of the battle—the remainder fled. Several radios (still switched on), telephones and a mass of cable suggested that the position had included a battalion head-quarters. Once again, as A and B Companies started to dig in, an accurate and fairly intense enemy artillery bombardment began, and in fact continued for some nine hours.

Following the success of A and B Companies, D Company crossed its second start line at the West end of the main ridge, while the light tanks and the machine-guns moved to a flank to give covering fire. The ridge itself was a long spire broken in the middle, with each section some 900 yards (300m) in length. The first feature was taken unopposed and there was then a short delay while the British artillery readjusted to its targets for the next phase. During this time the second feature was kept under heavy fire by the light tanks, the machine-guns and the MILAN missile being used in a direct-fire artillery role!

Just as the attack was about to start the commanding officer received a new piece of intelligence, that instead of one enemy company at the other end of the ridge there were two! This was hardly likely to impress the Paras who by this stage of the campaign had estab-lished a considerable moral ascend-

Above: British paratroops search captured Argentine soldiers in the 1982 South Atlantic war.

Right: Paras on the Falkland Islands manning a 7.62mm GPMG mounted on a tripod in the sustained fire role.

ency over the Argentines, but in the early minutes of this final phase of the battle D Company did receive some casualties as the enemy fought back with unexpect-ed vigour, withdrawing one bunker at a time. As the paras poured onto the position, however, the enemy suddenly broke and ran, being continuously harassed off the position by the machine-guns of the British Scorpions and Scimitars, and chased by the exhilarated paras.

As D Company began to re-organise they, too, came under artillery fire, as well as remarkably effective small arms fire from Tumbledown Mountain and Mount William to the South, which had not yet been captured by 5 Infantry Brigade. The enemy could be heard trying to regroup in the darkness below the ridge, and to the south in the area of Moody Brook. At daybreak a rather brave, but somewhat pathetic counter-attack developed from the area of Moody Brook, which seems to have been some sort of final gesture. It petered out within a few minutes under a hail of artillery, small arms and machine-gun fire.

This seems to have been the signal to many Argentines that the game was up, and shortly afterwards ever-increasing numbers of disheartened and disillusioned Argentine soldiers were observed streaming off Mount William, Tumbledown and Sapper Hill to seek an apparent (but very short-lived) refuge in Port Stanley. A and B Companies of 2 Para were now brought forward onto Wireless Ridge, and the battalion's night attack was successfully concluded. The paras had lost three dead and 11 wounded. Lack of time and opportunity precluded counting the Argentine casualties, but it has been estimated that, of an original strength of some 500, up to 100 may have been killed, 17 were captured, and the remainder fled.

The taking of Wireless Ridge illustrates the standards achieved by a crack unit. In this night battle it totally defeated a force of equal strength, well prepared and dug-in, and occupying a dominant feature. No. 2 Para had been through the traumatic experience of the Goose Green battle earlier in the campaign, but had learned the lessons well. They had also given the lie to the allegation that parachute units do not have "staying power". It is, perhaps, unfortunate that the battle of Goose Green, deservedly famous, has overshadowed this later minor classic at Wireless Ridge.

Royal Marines Special Boat Squadron

To a large extent the whole of the Royal Marines is an elite force in itself; every marine would certainly claim it so. However, the Royal Marines are basically very highly trained infantry, optimised for the amphibious role.

Within the Royal Marines there are a number of smaller and more select groups of which the best known and most highly trained is the Special Boat Squadron (SBS). This squadron has its roots in the special units raised in World War II for raiding and reconnaissance on the shores of the European mainland. The techniques evolved so painfully in war were, fortunately, preserved in peace, despite many cutbacks and amalgamations. The Amphibious School of the Royal Marines at Eastney (now at Poole in Dorset) included a "Small Raids Wing", which was later redesig-nated the "Special Boat Company" and then, in 1977, the "Special Boat Squadron".

The SBS is the headquarters for the Special Boat Sections which are deployed under the operational command of Commando units, but can also act autonomously on special tasks. The major role of the SBS is in amphibious operations, especially on reconnaissance, sabotage and demolitions. They are also believed to have particular responsibilities in the security of Britain's off-shore oil and gas rigs.

The SBS has seen action in the Oman, Borneo and the Falkland Islands War. In the latter the SBS were early ashore on South Georgia, having flown from the UK in a C-130 and then parachuted to a submarine in the South Atlantic. The submarine then took them close inshore and they then com-

Press Association

Special combat uniform with hood

Silenced Sterling SMG

Folding canvas canoe

9mm L34A1 Sterling sub-machine gun with silencer

Foresight

Above: A two-man SBS patrol coming ashore in a canvas folding canoe. They are wearing special camouflage suits and are carrying 9mm L34A1 Sterling sub-machine guns fitted with large silencers.

Left: Men of the SBS, the Royal Marines' elite unit, emerge from the hatch of a submarine during training. The ability to deliver men from a submarine onto a hostile shore is very valuable and was used on a number of occasions during the South Atlantic War of 1982.

pleted their long journey in inflatable Gemini boats. The SBS is also rumoured to have put patrols ashore on the Argentine mainland, landing from the conventional submarine, HMS *Onyx*, although this has never been confirmed. The SBS and SAS operated on the Falkland Islands long before the amphibious landings, and the SBS reconnoitred the actual landing sites at San Carlos Bay. They were there to welcome the first landing-craft to reach the shore, and also silenced the Argentinian outpost on Fanning Head, overlooking the landings. ▶

► The way in which the SBS fits in with the much larger SAS organisation is a matter for speculation, particularly as the SAS is known to have a Boat Troop, with similar equipment and capabilities to the SBS. Nevertheless, there is no known friction between the two units, and it must therefore be assumed that the responsibilities are not a problem in practice.

Selection and training

Recruitment to the SBS is from volunteers serving in the Royal Marine Commandos. All such officer and marine volunteers undergo the usual physical and psychological tests, followed by a three-week selection test. Successful candidates then go on a 15-week training course in seamanship, navigation, demolition, diving and advanced weapons handling. They then do a four-week parachute course, following which they join an operational Special Boat Section.

SBS officers and marines are not compelled to leave the SBS after a set period, as, for example, in the SAS, but like some other special forces they are usually forced to leave if they wish to obtain promotion past a certain point.

Uniforms

The SBS wear standard Royal Marine uniform and the commando green beret. The only indication in parade and barrack dress that a man belongs to the SBS is the wearing of Royal Marine parachuting wings on the right shoulder and of the "Swimmer Canoeist" badge on the right forearm. The latter has a crown above the letters "SC", flanked by laurel leaves. In parade dress both badges are embroidered in gold on a black backing. Officers of the SBS wear the wings, but not the "SC" badge (even though they are qualified to wear it by having passed the course).

Weapons and equipment

The SBS four-man patrols are usually armed with the US M16 Armalite rifle and M203 grenade launchers, although a special silenced version of the British Sterling sub-machine-gun (L34A1) is also used. Included in the patrol's equipment are plastic explosives, laser designators and burst-transmission radios. Extensive survival kits are also carried.

Boats used by the SBS include paddle-boards, specially-produced

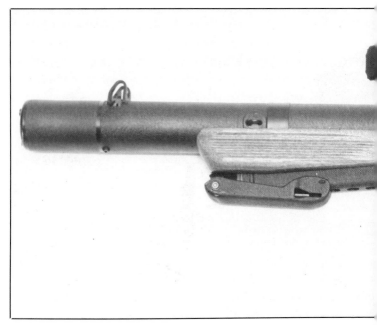

Klepper Mark 13 collapsible boats, and the somewhat larger Gemini boats powered by 40bhp outboard motors. The SBS can also be transported by "Rigid Raider" boats, a militarised version of the glassfibre "Dory" fishing-boat, powered by outboards of up to 140bhp, and operated by the specialists of the Royal Marines' Rigid Raider Squadron.

Above: Marines of the SBS on a training exercise. Continuous experience since 1941 makes them one of the world's best trained canoe forces.

Below: 9mm L34A1 Sterling sub-machine gun, a favourite weapon of the SBS. The wooden grip is needed as the barrel casing becomes too hot to hold.

Special Air Services

In December 1975 a four-man "Active-Service Unit" of the Provisional IRA was cornered by London's Metropolitan Police in a flat in Balcombe Street, in the capital's Marylebone area. The four Irishmen held the owners—an understandably terrified couple—hostage, and the police were faced with the problem of resolving matters without physical harm coming to the elderly pair. The "Provos" were confident that they could strike a bargain with the police sooner or later. It was known that there was a radio receiver in the flat and, during a routine news broadcast, the BBC announced that an armed section of the SAS had arrived at the scene of the siege. Shortly afterwards the Provos surrendered; the police they could cope with, but the SAS—they were something else!

Foundation

The SAS was formed early in World War II, at a time when many "special" units were being raised, by Lt. David Stirling, who was then serving with No. 8 Commando, a British Army unit. Known originally as "L Detachment", by October 1942 the unit had grown to 390 men and it was redesignated 1st Special Air Service Regiment (1 SAS). After various reorganisations and a period of further growth, an SAS Brigade was formed in Scotland in January 1944, consisting of two British regiments (1 and 2 SAS), two French regiments (3 and 4 SAS), a Belgian squadron (later 5 SAS) and a signal squadron.

The SAS fought throughout the Desert campaign, in Italy and in Northwest Europe, establishing a reputation for independent action by small groups of very highly trained men, operating deep behind enemy lines. At the end of the war in Europe the British Army divested itself of "private armies" with indecent haste, and the SAS were among those to go. No. 5 SAS was handed over to the Belgian Army in September 1945, followed by 3 and 4 SAS which were transferred

to the French Army a month later. A week after this HQ SAS and 1 and 2 SAS were disbanded, and it appeared that the British Army had washed its hands of the "SAS idea", altogether and for ever.

It takes more than that to keep a good idea down, however, and within months it was decided that there would be a role for SAS-type activities in a future war in Europe. This led to the conversion of a Territorial Army (TA) unit, "The Artists' Rifles", into 21st Special Air Service Regiment (21 SAS) (Artists) —(Volunteers), the number 21 being obtained by taking the numbers of the two British wartime SAS regiments (1 and 2 SAS), combining and reversing them.

One of the early British post-war anti-colonial campaigns was the Malayan "Emergency" (1948-60). Brigadier Michael Calvert, a renowned ex-Chindit and commander of the SAS Brigade 1944-45, arrived in Malaya in 1951 and formed the "Malayan Scouts (Special Air Service)" which quickly built up to regimental size. In 1952 the Malayan Scouts were redesignated 22nd Special Air Service Regiment (22 SAS), thus marking the official return of the SAS to the regular army's order of battle. The reputation of the SAS in Malaya was second to none. They spent very long periods in the deep jungle where they established particularly close links with the aboriginal peoples, and they also pioneered the techniques for parachuting into the trees and then abseiling down long ropes to the jungle floor.

When the conflict in Malaya began to wind-down, the SAS were sent to the Oman in the Arabian peninsula in November/December 1958, where they carried out a daring attack on rebels in the 8,000ft (2,500m) high Jebel ▶

Right: An SAS trooper on patrol during the South Atlantic war. During this campaign the SAS proved that they are as good in conventional war as they are at dealing with terrorists.

"Bergen" rucksack

Cold weather combat hat

"Sweat rag" used as a scarf

Belts of 7.62mm ball ammunition

7.62mm L7A2 general-purpose machine-gun

British Army pattern camouflaged combat uniform

Canvas anklets

British Army DMS boots

97

► Akhdar, totally defeating the Arab dissidents in their own home ground. Following this success, 22 SAS moved to the UK where, after a short period in Malvern, they settled down in their now-famous home base at Bradbury Lines, Hereford. But by now they had been reduced to an HQ and two "sabre" squadrons.

The Far East soon beckoned again, however, with the "Confrontation Campaign" in Borneo, and a squadron of SAS arrived there in January 1963. Their success led to more demands for SAS and the third squadron had to be re-formed in mid-1963. This was just as well, because war broke out in Aden and from 1964-66 the three squadrons of 22 SAS were rotating between the UK, Borneo and Aden in a period known in the regiment as the "happy time". By 1967 these two wars were over and the SAS had a short period of consolidation and retraining.

In 1969 the situation in Northern Ireland suddenly exploded and the SAS began a long acquaintanceship with the Province. Simultaneously, renewed problems in Malaya and the Oman led to a return there. In July 1972, at the Battle of Mirbat in Oman, ten SAS soldiers, aided by a few local soldiers, defeated 250 dissidents in a memorable engagement. The SAS remained in the Oman for many years and there may be a few members there still. In August 1983 it was disclosed that the SAS was training a similar unit for the Sultan of Oman's "Special Force", composed of parachutists trained to exist for days on little food in desert conditions.

The anti-guerrilla campaigns of the 1950s, 1960s and early 1970s were succeeded by a new role in which the SAS quickly built up an unrivalled expertise — counter-terrorist actions. Spurred on by operations in Northern Ireland against the Irish Republican Army (IRA) and Irish National Liberation Army (INLA) the SAS has developed techniques which are copied throughout the Western world. This has led to the SAS not only being consulted by overseas governments and special forces, but

also in being directly involved in some "foreign" operations. Thus, in October 1977, two SAS men were with the West German GSG 9 unit at the attack to recapture a hijacked German airliner at Mogadishu, and SAS members were also involved in the earlier Dutch operation against the Moluccan terrorists who had taken over a train-load of hostages.

Most famous of all such episodes, however, was the London Iranian Embassy siege of May 1980 when the SAS had perforce to conduct the operation in front of the world's TV cameras. In strict compliance with English law, the Metropolitan Police conducted the operation until the terrorists murdered one of the hostages and threw his body out on the street. The police then requested the SAS to take over, and the troops stormed

in, using special weapons and tactics, and rescued all the remaining hostages. All but one of the terrorists was killed.

This spectacular success, while a god-send for the hero-hungry world media, gave the SAS far more publicity than the Service would have preferred.

By 1982 the SAS seemed to be settled in their counter-terrorist role when, to everyone's surprise, the Falklands War with Argentina broke out. No. 22 SAS were immediately involved and were given the opportunity to remind the world that they are first and foremost professional soldiers, trained for war. They spearheaded the return to South Georgia island, although the first reconnaissance landing in helicopters had to be aborted in truly appalling weather. The second landing was by inflat-

Above: SAS troopers training in a desert environment. The "target" on the left is wearing the SAS sand-coloured beret and the special camouflage smock used by SAS and SBS.

able boats and most men got ashore. One boat, however, broke down and the soldiers refused to compromise the operation by calling for help on the radio and were blown rapidly eastwards; by the greatest of good fortune they hit the very tip of the island and were later rescued by helicopter. Meanwhile, at Grytviken, squadron headquarters and one troop of D Squadron took advantage of the crippling of the Argentine submarine "Santa Fe" to rush in and overwhelm the garrison, and South Georgia was quickly back under British control. ▶

99

▶ The first SAS soldiers were ashore on East Falklands by May 1 and remained there, close to the enemy and in foul weather, for some thirty days. They provided vital intelligence on troop movements and deployments, and also targetted enemy aircraft and stores for aircraft strikes and naval gunfire support. On May 14th, the SAS raided Pebble Island and blew up 11 Argentine aircraft, a reversion to their original role in the North African desert 40 years previously. It is also reported that they operated on the mainland of Argentina itself, although this has never been officially confirmed.

After victory in the Falklands War, the SAS continued to receive a great deal of unhelpful media attention. The regiment's continued role in the war against terrorism guaranteed it a notoriety among IRA sympathisers. The successful interception and killing of three IRA member in Gibralter led to a chorus of naive and fatuous criticism.

In 1991 the SAS found themselves back in the desert — working in close co-ordination with the US Special Forces, above all with *Delta Force* in the hunt for Iraq's "Scud" missiles. SAS teams attacked Iraqi missile storage facilities and command and control centres. Others used hand-held laser designators to iluminate key targets for Allied laser-guided munitions.

Organisation

The present organisation includes three regiments of approximately 600 to 700 men each. One regiment (22 SAS) is all-regular, while the other two (21 SAS (Artists rifles) and 23 SAS) belong to the Territorial Army. There is a regular signal squadron with 22 SAS and another (63 (SAS) Signal Squadron) with the TA. These units are controlled by Director SAS Group, a brigadier whose headquarters are in London.

Although they no longer operate together the SAS maintains close links with the New Zealand Special Air Service Squadron and the Australian Special Air Service. Fraternal links are also maintained with the 1st Parachute Battalion of the Belgian Army which is descended from the wartime 5 SAS, and the Greek "Sacred Squadron (Helios Lokos)" which served with the SAS in North Africa and the Eastern Mediterranean during the last war.

There is a very close relationship between the present-day regular (22 SAS) and territorial (21 and 23 SAS) regiments. Both territorial regiments have a strong cadre of

Below: SAS trooper crossing a fence on the Brecon Beacons in Wales. Rifle is an old FN FAL used only for training (DP on the butt denotes "Drill Purpose").

Press Association

regulars, who ensure that professional standards are maintained, and who pass on the benefits of recent operational experience.

Selection and training

No officer or soldier enlists directly into the regular regiment (22 SAS). Instead, volunteers come from the other regiments and corps of the British Army, which sometimes leads to the accusation that the regiment is "poaching" some of the best and most enterprising young officers and soldiers. All volunteers for the SAS must first pass the selection course, which is based on the regimental depot at Hereford. The tests take place in the Brecon area of Wales and consist of a series of tasks designed to find out whether the individual has the qualities of mental resilience, physical stamina, self-discipline and spiritual toughness which the regiment has found necessary for its missions.

The process starts with 10 days of fitness and map-reading training in groups of 20 to bring everyone up to the same basic standards. This is followed by 10 days of solitary cross-country marching, culminating in a 40 mile (64km) march in 20 hours carrying a 55lb

Above: Volunteers for the SAS have to show not only physical and mental ability, but also basic military skills.

(25kg) Bergen rucksack. Those who have not either voluntarily or compulsorily retired now undertake 14 weeks continuation training which includes a parachute course and combat survival training. At the end of this phase the survivors are presented with their beret and badge, and are at long last members of the SAS, although the training continues with specialist courses in signalling, languages, field medicine, demolition, shooting, free-fall parachuting and other military skills. It is only after some two years that a soldier can be considered to be a fully-fledged member of the regiment, and even then there can be periods of high-intensity training for roles such as counter-revolutionary warfare commandos.

Unlike the earlier years of the SAS the emphasis today is on pulling and encouraging men to get through the tests and course, but without in any way relaxing the high standards. Nevertheless, the pass-rate is only about 20 per cent, although it must be appreciated ▶

▶ that only rarely is there any reason for any of the other 80 per cent to feel ashamed; the fact is that the SAS are, of necessity, looking for a very special combination of talents which is possessed by or can be developed in only a few people.

Once fully in the regiment the regular officers' and soldiers' normal tour of duty is three years, following which they will usually return to their parent regiment or corps. This ensures that the regiment does not become too introspective and also serves to spread around the rest of the Army that curious blend of ideas and training which constitute the SAS.

Weapons and equipment

The SAS are constantly testing new weapons and equipment for their many specialist roles. In addition to the standard range of British infantry weapons, the regiment has recently adopted SiG-Sauer 9mm pistols in place of its trusted Browning P35s. Their most famous weapon is the Heckler and Koch MP5 9mm sub-machine-gun which was used to such good effect during the storming of the Iranian Embassy. Other exotic weapons evaluated in recent years include .50in calibre sniper rifles; these can disable aircraft, bring down helicopters and even penetrate the armour of light vehicles. They have also been used to detonate unexploded bombs from a safe distance. The squadrons take turns in the Counter Revolutionary Warfare role: ready to don the now familiar black assault suit and gas mask. This kit has been substantially revised since the Embassy raid and includes "Flashbang" stun grenades,

The Iranian Embassy Siege   April 30-May 5 1980

The siege of the Iranian Embassy in London in April—May 1980 caught the imagination of the world and brought the SAS into the limelight because the denouement took place before the gathered Press photographers and TV. The eerie, black-clad figures, their efficiency and the success and sheer drama of the event established the SAS a public reputation and created an expectation of success which will endure for many years.

The Iranian Embassy at No. 16 Princes Gate, London, opposite Hyde Park, was taken over at 1130 hours Wednesday April 30 by six terrorists, armed with three 9mm automatic pistols, one 0.38in revolver, two 9mm sub-machine guns and a number of Chinese-made hand-grenades. There were six men directly involved: Oan, the leader (27 years old), and five others, all in their early twenties. They were all from Arabistan, an area of Iran some 400 miles (643km) from Teheran, which had long resisted the rule of the Aryan northerners. Most had supported Ayatollah Khomeini's takeover from the Shah, only to find him as ruthless a suppressor of minorities as his predecessor. The terrorists represented a group entitled the Democratic Revolutionary Movement for the Liberation of Arabistan (DRMLA), a Marxist-Leninist group based in Libya, whose cause was regional autonomy (not independence) for Arabistan.

The occupants of the Embassy at the time of the takeover numbered 29: four British and 22 Iranian men and women, three of whom escaped during the early minutes. The terrorists' demands were initially that 91 prisoners in Arabistan be released by the Iranian authorities. The deadline was set for 1200 hours Thursday May 1, and during that night the terrorists had the first of many contacts with the London police and the media.

One sick Iranian woman was released late on the Wednesday night and a sick Englishman the following morning. The first deadline was postponed when the police transmitted a message from ▶

Right: Two SAS men outside the Iranian Embassy in London during the brief action which ended the siege. They are aiming 9mm High-Power Browning pistols, but have a rifle and tear gas launcher ready at their feet

body armour, knives and shotguns in addition to pistols and sub-machine-guns.

Uniform

The SAS deliberately shuns glamorous or flashy uniforms or embellishments, and wears standard British Army uniforms, as far as possible, with only the customary "regimental" items permitted under British practice. The three basic distinguishing marks of the SAS are the sand-coloured beret, the cap-badge (a winged dagger with the motto "Who Dares Wins") and SAS "wings" worn on the right shoulder. In parade dress (No. 2 Dress) the buttons, officers' Sam Browne belt, gloves and shoes are all black. Combat dress is standard British Army pattern with either the sand-coloured beret or the peaked camouflage hat with no badge. With this latter hat on there is nothing about a soldier's uniform to show that he is a member of the SAS at all. One small idiosyncracy of SAS uniform is that in "pullover order" (the popular dress worn in barracks) the chevrons of NCO, are worn on the shoulder straps, not on the right sleeve.

A unique combat uniform is available for use on anti-terrorist operations. This is an all-black outfit, with a black flak-vest, belt and boots. The standard issue respirator (which is made of black rubber) and grey anti-flash hood complete the outfit. Every item of this dress is worn for strictly practical reasons, but the overall effect is awe-inspiring, as was demonstrated during the Iranian Embassy rescue in May 1980.

London Express

▶ the terrorists to the Press, and a second deadline (1400 hours) passed without a move from either side.

By the Friday morning there had been numerous contacts between the terrorists and the police, some direct and some through intermediaries, but by now specific threats were being made against the lives of the hostages. Negotiations continued throughout the Saturday and a major advance was achieved when the terrorists agreed to release two hostages in return for a broadcast on the radio of a statement of their aims. One hostage was released in the early evening and after the statement had been broadcast on the BBC 2100 hours news, word for word as given by the terrorist leader to the police, a further hostage was released. The atmosphere in the Embassy became almost euphoric, helped by a good meal sent in by the police.

Through the Sunday the British Government discussed the situation with various Arab ambassadors, but no agreement could be reached on a possible role for them in reaching a resolution to the crisis. In the Embassy the major event in an anti-climactic day was the release of an Iranian hostage who had become very ill. On Monday the terrorists were noticeably more nervous and a shouted discussion between two British hostages and the police at noon did little to ease the tension. At about 1330 Oan's patience apparently snapped and he shot Abbas Lavasani, one of the Embassy staff, in the course of a telephone discussion with the police. This was the turning point.

Any doubts about whether anyone had actually been killed were resolved just after 1900 when the dead body was pushed through the front door of the Embassy and a pair of policemen rushed forward and carried it away on a stretcher.

SAS soldiers had visited the scene on the first day of the siege, and thereafter they stood-by in an Army barracks some two miles away. The police had obviously tried their best to identify just where the hostages and their captors were and what they were all doing, and many highly classified surveillance devices were used. The SAS were therefore as ready as it was possible to be in the circumstances when, in accordance with British legal practice, the police formally asked the military to deal with the situation.

The rescue

The plan was to use just 12 men in three teams of the customary four-man SAS groups; two teams were to take the rear, descending by rope from the roof, one team to reach the ground and the second the first-floor balcony. Both would then break-in using either frame-charges or brute force. Team three was to be at the front, crossing from a balcony at No. 15 Princes Gate to No. 16. Once inside all three teams were to rush to reach the hostages before they could be harmed.

Everything that could be done to heighten the impact of the attack was done. The 12 SAS men were dressed from head to foot in black, even including rubber anti-gas respirators, and looked extremely menacing. They would gain entrance using 4ft x 2ft (1.2 x 0.6m) frame charges, followed by stun grenades ("flash-bangs"). CS gas would also be used. The combination of explosions, noise, smoke, speed of action and the appearance of the men was all intended to strike confusion and dread into the minds of the terrorists —and succeeded brilliantly.

The SAS men had, naturally, pored over the plans of the building in minute detail and had also spent many hours studying the photographs of the hostages. But, in the end—as every soldier knows—all the training and planning have to be translated into action.

At 1926 hours precisely the men of the rear attack force stepped over the edge of the roof and abseiled down. The first two went down each rope successfully, but one of the third pair became stuck, a hazard known to abseilers everywhere. In the front SAS men appeared on the balcony of No. 15 and climbed over to the Embassy,

Press Association

giving the world's Press and the public an image of their regiment which will last for years.

Simultaneously the police spoke to the terrorists on the telephone and distracted their attention at the critical moment that the SAS suddenly broke in. Stun grenades exploded, lights went out and all was noise and apparent confusion. Some parts of the Embassy caught fire and the SAS man caught on the rope at the rear was cut free and dropped onto a balcony—a risk preferable to that of being roasted alive.

The SAS men swept through the Embassy. Two terrorists were quickly shot and killed. One started shooting the hostages in an upstairs

Above: The image of the SAS that shook the world. These men wear black uniforms and boots, standard respirators and NBC hoods. Their weapon is the Heckler & Koch 9mm MP5 sub-machine gun.

room, but stopped after causing a few wounds. Within minutes five of the six gunmen were dead, with the sixth sheltering among the newly-freed hostages. All survivors were rushed downstairs into the garden, where the remaining terrorist was identified and arrested. Not one hostage was killed in the attack, which was, quite simply, a major success in the West's fight against the evils of terrorism.

Special Operations Forces

In April 1980, a catalogue of disasters led to the failure of Operation *Eagle Claw*, an ambitious attempt to rescue the American hostages held in Iran. The reputation of the US armed forces' elite formations dropped to an all-time low. Yet little more than ten years later, US special operations troops were credited by General H. Norman Schwarzkopf with keeping Israel out of the Gulf War and making other vital contributions to the success of the Coalition strategy. Operation *Desert Storm* finally vindicated the US special warfare units. So prominent during the Vietnam War, they fell into disfavour as the United States admitted defeat in South-East Asia. There was even opposition from within the Army: many senior officers had no time for the theories of unconventional warfare once so very fashionable during John F. Kennedy's presidency.

The tragic failure of the raid on Tehran led to a drastic revision of US special operations policy. Men and units that had languished in the wilderness since Vietnam were returned to duty. Above all, the Army, Navy and Air Force accepted the need to permanently link their various elite units, recognising that the *ad hoc* nature of the Tehran rescue force was a major factor in its failure. Today, the Joint Chiefs of Staff are advised by the Joint Special Operations Agency on all situations that may require the commitment of special warfare units. Since 1988 all such units, whether Army, Navy or Air Force, have been under the control of the US Special Operations Command (USSOC) based at McDill Air Force Base in Tampa, Florida. USSOC directs operations in five commands: Special Operations Pacific, Special Operations Atlantic, Special Operations Central, Special Operations South and Special Operations Europe.

Army special units

All US Army special warfare units come under the control of 1st Special Operations Command based at Fort Bragg in North Carolina. The units are:

● **Special Forces**

In the US Army the term "special forces" refers to a discrete unit, also popularly known as the Green Berets. Its motto, *De Oppresso Liber* (To Liberate From Oppression)

Below: Near their home base at Hurlburt Field, Florida, men of the 1st SOW combat control team are seen undertaking amphibious warfare training in the Everglades swampland.

Above: The immense value of being able to insert covert operations teams deep inside enemy territory is reflected in the importance placed by the majority of SOF's on the art of parachuting. Note the low level of this drop.

expresses the Special Forces' role in nurturing and leading resistance movements behind enemy lines.

● **Eskimo Scouts**
Part of Alaska's Army National Guard, this 1,500-man unit is divided between the trio of ARNG's reconnaissance battalions. It is responsible for training personnel from other special units in the skills of Arctic warfare.

● **75th Ranger Regiment**
Consisting of three battalions and a recon team, the Rangers are elite light infantry who form a pool of highly-trained individuals from which many other special units draw their personnel. Two battalions were formed in the wake of the 1973 Arab-Israeli War and a third was added in 1984 after their success in Grenada. In 1987 these battalions became the 75th Infantry Regiment (Ranger) and received the lineage and honours won by the Ranger units during World War II and the Korean War.

● **Long-Range Surveillance Groups**
Successors to the LRRPs in Vietnam, these companies of reconnaissance troops were added to US forces in Germany during the 1980s. It was a belated recognition that, in sharp contrast to neighbouring British and German divisions, the US Corps in West Germany had no long-range patrol capabiliy at all.

● **Special Operations Aviation Brigade**
This is a helicopter unit dedicated to transporting special warfare detachments into and out of action. It includes the 160th Aviation Battalion, formerly a "Black" (i.e. secret) unit of helicopter gunships and assault helicopters.

● **"Seapsray"**
A covert Army-Central Intelligence Agency unit that provides clandestine transport for secret operations worldwide.

● **Intelligence Support Agency**
A shadowy organization with an intelligence-gathering remit similar to that of the Defense Intelligence Agency.

● **122nd Signals Battalion**
Responsible for all communications links between US Army special warfare units.

● **96th Civil Affairs Group**
Performs Civil-Military relations in areas where special units are operational.

● **4th Psychological Operations (PSYOPS) Group**
Four battalions dedicated to psychological warfare.

Navy special units

The US Navy includes two Naval Special Warfare Groups: NSWG 1, based at Coronado, California, supports naval operations in the Pacific; NSWG 2, based at Little

Creek, Virginia, supports the US Atlantic Fleets. Several units are based abroad e.g. the SEAL team and special warfare unit at RAF Machrihanish in Scotland. The US Navy's NSWGs include:

●Sea Air Land Teams (SEAL)

These grew out of the earlier Underwater Demolition Teams and have established a well-earned reputation as one of the most professional special warfare units in the world. Tasked with a wide variety of missions, the SEALs are well supported by the US Navy which has converted one Sturgeon and two Ethan Allen class nuclear submarines to carry up to 80 SEALs into action. They carry Swimmer Delivery Vehicles — mini-submarines which allow the SEALs to make clandestine landings on enemy-held coastlines.

●SEAL Team Six

This is a reinforced SEAL team dedicated to anti-terrorist operations created in November 1980. It is integrated with the Army's anti-terrorist organisation and can be considered the naval component of *Delta Force*. Operating under Joint Special Operations Command control, it is trained and equipped to deal with incidents like the hijacking of the *Achille Lauro*. Based at Dam Neck near Norfolk, Virginia, it works closely with the Royal Marines' Special Boat Squadron.

●US Marine Corps

The US Marine Corps have a pair of reconnaissance units: Reconnaissance Battalions and the Force Reconnaissance Companies (also known as Force Recon). Each of the three USMC divisions includes an elite Reconnaissance Battalion and each regular battalion is assigned a Force Recon company. The USMC also includes Fleet Anti-Terrorist Teams which are deployed to protect base facilities against terrorist attack or sabotage.

US Air Force

All USAF unconventional warfare units are controlled by the Air Force Special Operations Command. This replaced the 23rd Air Force, created in 1983 when special warfare and search-and-rescue formations were merged. USAF special operations units include:

●1st Special Operations Wing

Based at Hulburt Field, Florida, this directs the Special Operations Squadrons (SOS) which are trained to fly special warfare units in behind enemy lines, supply them and extract them when required. Three are based in the USA, one in the Philippines, one in Germany and one in the UK.

●Air Reserve and Air National Guard SOS

These include the 919th Special Operations Group (SOG) (AC-130 gunships) and the 302nd SOG (EC-130E command and control aircraft) as well as the Pennsylvania Air National Guard's 193rd SOG (EC-130E PSYOPS aircraft).

●1723rd Combat Control Squadron

Often attached to Army Special Forces units, this formation receives training similar to that of the Special Forces and acts a Pathfinder force, selecting and marking landing zones and controlling airborne special operations.

Above: To an outsider, life in the SOF's may appear to be glamorous, but the reality is quite different. Challenges both physical and mental are common, and only the best of the best will ever make it through the training regime that selects the "elite".

Below: The inflatable boat small (IBS) is a key element in the SEAL inventory, and this muscle-straining IBS exercise is central to the SEAL training programme. A small outboard engine can be used to enhance waterborne travel on covert missions into enemy territory.

US Air Force Special Operations Command

The loss of a single AC-130H "Spectre" gunship during the battle for Khafji was the first open indication that the US Air Force's Special Operations Squadrons (SOS) were active during the Gulf War. In fact, it was on the word of a USAF Colonel that General Schwarskopf initiated Operation *Desert Storm* in the way he did. Baghdad was protected by a chain of Soviet-supplied radar stations that were electronically linked in pairs — so an attack on one would immediately alert its neighbour. Colonel George A. Gray, commanding 1st Special Operations Wing (SOW) stated that the "Pave Low" helicopters of the 20th SOS could penetrate Iraqi airspace without detection and guide Army AH-64A Apache gunships to appropriate firing positions. Two adjacent radar systems could then be destroyed *simultaneously* using Hellfire guided missiles. This would create a gap in the enemy defences through which the main air attack would go in, preceded by F-117A Stealth fighter-bombers tasked with neutralising the Iraqi surface-to-air missile (SAM) sites and command and control centres.

The MH-53H "Pave Low IIIs" crossed the Iraqi border at an altitude of about 50ft (15.25m) during the early hours of 17 January 1991. The entire operation worked as advertised, with the two sites being destroyed within two seconds of the planned time.

Army Special Forces were keen to enter Iraq before the Coalition offensive began. Indeed, the Green Berets pressed to send teams to stir up the rebellion in Kurdistan and southern Iraq in their own inimitable way. However, the Administration decided to rely solely on CIA activity before hostilities began. As soon as *Desert Shield* became *Desert Storm*, Special Forces teams were flown deep into Iraq by elements of the 1st SOW. Some personnel were inserted by "Pave Low" helicopters while other teams were landed by MC-130E "Combat Talon Is". During the great "Scud hunt", Special Forces teams raced around the west of Iraq in "dune buggy" cross-country vehicles. Looking more at home in a *Mad Max* movie

Below: Late in the night and at low-level, one of the 20th SOS's Sikorsky MH-53J "Pave Low III" helicopters, as seen through Night Vision Goggles.

than a real army, they gave SF teams the vital ability to cover long distances quickly. All this activity depended on complete and thorough co-ordination of ground and air special warfare units.

The "Combat Talon" cargo aircraft demonstrated their flexibility by acting as bombers during the Gulf War. In an operation co-ordinated with the Army Special Force's 4th Psychological Warfare Group, the 8th SOS dropped a total of eleven BLU-82s 15,000lb (6,801kg) bombs. These are the largest non-nuclear bombs in the world and were also used during the Vietnam War to create instant helicopter landing zones in dense jungle. The monstrous explosions were advertised

Above: One of SOC's AC-130 "Spectre" gunship opens up on an enemy target with its 20mm Gatling guns. Note the sensor pods along the fuselage side.

Below: MC-130E flying very low in rough terrain. Pilots fly their machines like fighters, even though they were built as long-range transports.

in advance by millions of leaflets and followed by the huge mushroom cloud of a BLU-82 detonating. One collapsed all Iraqi bunkers in a three-mile (4.8km) radius and these tremendous explosions left many Iraqis with no will to fight. A British SAS patrol behind Iraqi lines

▶ reportedly radioed its headquarters when it saw the first one and reported that 'they've just nuked Kuwait!' The BLU-82s were usually dropped in pairs from 17,000ft (5,185m) to avoid anti-aircraft fire. The two MC-130s involved were soon nicknamed "the Blues Brothers".

Organisation

The 1st SOW comprises:

●8th Special Operations Squadron

This is equipped with MC-130E "Combat Talon Is": a specialised variant of the Lockheed C-130 Hercules four-engined transport aircraft. Unarmed, slow and unmanoeuverable, the MC-130s rely on their APQ-122 terrain-following/terrain-avoidance (TF/TA) radar to let them operate at or below 250ft (76.25m). Flying *around* hills rather than over them, these aircraft exploit every fold in the ground to remain below the horizon of enemy radar. The delivery or re-supply of Special Forces teams requires the same accuracy as precision bombing — small groups of soldiers behind enemy lines cannot clearly mark their position and most oeprations must be carried out under cover of darkness. Using its High-Speed, Low-Level Airborne Delivery System (HSLLADS), an MC-130 can drop 622lb (1,000kg) pallets with great accuracy while travelling at nearly 345mph (555.60km/h) and only 250ft (76.25m). The MC-130Es were supposed to have been supple-

mented by an improved version, designated MC-130H "Combat Talon II" by 1987. However, with nine successive managers in seven years, this programme is years behind schedule and costs have soared to \$2.47 billion for 24 aircraft! The first "Combat Talon II" is now expected to enter service in 1992.

●16th Special Operations Squadron

This operates AC-130H "Spectre"

Below: A USAF pilot acts as the floating target for an Air Rescue Service helicopter on a SAR exercise in the Pacific Ocean.

gunships which are in the same basic configuration now as they were during the last days of the Vietnam War. There are two 20mm cannon in the forward part of the fuselage and a 40mm Bofors and a 105mm howitzer in the rear. All weapons fire from the aircraft's port side. Circling the target in a ''pylon turn'', it is capable of great accuracy and can fire its devastating armament on enemy forces located very close to friendly troops. Provided the enemy air threat is negligible and there are no concentrations of SAMs or anti-aircraft artillery (AAA), the AC-130

Above: The AC-130 ''Spectre'' gunship is by far and away the most awesome weapon in the SOC's aviation inventory.

is a valuable source of supporting fire for Special Forces detachments. Twelve much-improved AC-130Us were supposed to begin entering service during 1992, but this programme is running at least two years late.

Below: Teamwork is well to the fore in the cockpit of one of the 8th SOS's MC-130E's as it heads to the drop zone. ▶

● 20th Special Operations Squadron

This squadron is equipped with MH-53J "Pave Low III" helicopters. Originally built as Sikorsky HH-53 "Jolly Green Giant" combat rescue helicopters, eight have been fitted with TF/TA radar and Forward-Looking Infra-Red (FLIR) to help them fly at altitudes of less than 100ft (30.5m). Flying these $26 million helicopters is one of the most demanding missions in the USAF. The MH-53Js are modernised versions of the original MH-53Hs which were essentially 1960s

helicopters with a host of modern navigational devices imposed on their original instrumentation. The "Pave Low's" train for long sorties which often include inflight-refuelling at an altitude of less than 500ft (152.5m).

In addition to the 1st SOW, the USAF has several other speical warfare units deployed at bases around the world:

● 1st Special Operations Squadron

This small squadron of four MC-130Es was based at Clark AFB, Philippines, until the airbase was closed by the eruption of a nearby volcano in 1991.

● 7th Special Operations Squadron

Also comprising four MC-130Es, the 7th SOS is base at Rhein-Main AFB, Germany.

Below: An extremely versatile helicopter, the MH-53J "Pave Low III" can be used for any number of mission profiles, including maritime rescue.

●39th Special Operations Wing
Based at RAF Woodbridge, England, this consists of the 21st SOS which flies MH-53Js and the 67th SOS which operates HC-130N tanker/communications aircraft.

Air Rescue Service

The Air Rescue Service (ARS) was re-established in 1989 at McClellan AFB, California. Originally formed in 1946, it was part of Military Airlift Command until 1983 when the USAF agreed to disband it and allow Army helicopter units to take over its work. Disagreement within the Air Force and Congress led to the USAF creating the 23rd Air Force in 1983: a merger of its special warfare and rescue units and forerunner of Special Operations Command. Today, the ARS operates

Above: A total of 33 HH-53s and CH-53s are scheduled to be upgraded to MH-53J standard. This example, operated by the 20th SOS, is seen conducting an in-flight refuelling via a Lockheed HC-130N operated by the co-located 67th SOS.

UH-60s and HH-60Gs. The very capable HH-60D dedicated search-and-rescue helicopter was finally cancelled in 1985 after the cost had reached $21 million per copy.

Below: Another helicopter now making its mark in SOC is the MH-60G Pave Hawk, 20 of which are slated for assignment to ARS units. Note the prominent air-to-air refuelling probe offset to starboard.

Special Forces

The US Army Special Forces are widely referred to as the "Green Berets". They had a very high profile during the Vietnam war and suffered accordingly when the USA was defeated in South-East Asia. Units were disbanded and manning levels decreased until the terrorist threat of the late-1970s led to the creation of *Delta Force*. From the early-1980s the Army began to take a renewed interest in unconventional warfare and the Green Berets began to reform. The Special Forces proved themselves again during the 1991 Gulf War and the Army seems to have learned its lesson. As the overall defence budget is being pruned now that the Warsaw Pact has vanished, the Special Forces are not only immune from the cuts — they are actually expanding. From 1991, Special Operations Command has control of its own budget and it is just completing a major evaluation of unconventional warfare tactics for the 1990s. The Pentagon's Special Operations and Low intensity Conflict office has a $2.31 billion budget for 1991 and is requesting $3 billion for 1992.

The term "special forces" was originally used during World War II to denote British Special Operations Executive and American Office of Strategic Studies (OSS) personnel working behind enemy lines,

organising and supporting local resistance movements. General William J. "Wild Bill" Donovan's OSS was demobilised immediately after World War II, destroying the USA's ability to wage unconventional warfare at the stroke of a pen. This was the era of the "big battalions", atomic bombs and a pervasive anti-elitist mood in the US Army.

The Greek Civil War, insurrection in the Philippines and ultimately, the Korean War, led to a revival of Special Forces units — although many of the "manpower slots" were created by abolishing the 14 independent Ranger companies. In June 1952, the first volunteers assembled at Smoke Bomb Hill, Fort Bragg, North Carolina, to form the 10th Special Forces Group (Airborne). It was deployed to Germany after a year's training, ready to wage guerrilla war in Eastern Europe should it come to war with the Soviet Union and its Warsaw Pact allies.

Below: Special Forces training is rigorous and constant, and takes place within specially constructed courses at Army bases, such as this one at Fort Bragg, as well as "in the field" in a variety of terrains from desert to snow-covered mountains to swampland.

The Special Forces expanded rapidly after President John F. Kennedy became an enthusiastic supporter. The Green Beret — worn in contravention of Army regulations off and on since 1952 — was finally authorised. Their motto *De Oppressor Liber* (To Liberate From Oppression) appealed to Kennedy who saw the deployment of small numbers of highly-trained soldiers as the key to defeating communist guerrilla warfare in Asia. The 77th SFG(A) was formed from a cadre of 10th SFG(A) and sent to Laos

Above: A patrol of the US Army's Special Forces in close-country. After a post-Vietnam period of neglect the Special Forces (the "Green Berets") are now in vogue once again. A new HQ has been set up, new units formed and equipment bought, all spurred by events in Latin America.

to train the local forces there. The 5th SFG(A) was raised in 1961 with the 3rd, 7th and 8th following in succession in 1963.

In Vietnam the Green Berets led

117

▶ a profusion of local forces including various Vietnamese militia organisations, the hill tribes (Montagnards), Nung (ethnic Chinese) and Khmers. Learning local languages, operating far from the support of regular Army units, they took the war to the enemy, challenging the Viet Cong's control of the countryside. Many Green Beret operations were co-ordinated by Military Assistance Command Vietnam, Studies and Operations Group (MACV-SOG), often referred to as the Special Operations Group. This was a joint-service body that achieved far more with its irregular tactics than the Army's big battalions. Yet despite their success, many senior US officers remained opposed to what they regarded as scruffy individualists who "went native" in the jungle. Special Forces operations began to be phased out in 1970; the militia and tribal units so painstakingly developed were handed over to South Vietnamese control. MACV-SOG was deactivated in 1972.

Organisation

Unlike many of the World's special operations units, the Green Berets are divided into Groups which are trained and equipped to fight in

Above: A Group of Special Forces soldiers on a training exercise. The lead scout is carrying a 5.56mm Colt Commando, derived from the M16 but with a shorter barrel, larger flash suppressor and a telescopic butt. Only the Green Berets use this gun.

discrete operational theatres. The units that make up the US Army Special Forces today are:

● **1st Special Forces Operational Detachment** (see *Delta Force*).
● **1st Special Forces Group (Airborne)**
Dedicated to operations in North-East Asia and the Pacific Ocean. Includes a detachment based at Seoul, South Korea, which speaks many different Asian languages.
● **3rd Special Forces Group (Airborne)**
Based at Fort Bragg. Each SFG(A) consists of three battalions each of three companies of six 'A' teams.
● **5th Special Forces Group (Airborne)**
One of the SFG(A)s to survive the Vietnam War, the 5th took part in the *Bright Star* deployments to Egypt in the early-1980s and is now tailored for operations in the Indian Ocean and South-East Asia. The 5th

Organisation of Special Forces "A Team"

Commanding Officer:	Captain.
Executive Officer:	Lieutenant.
Operations Sergeant:	Sergeant (E8).
Heavy Weapons Leader:	Sergeant (E7).
Intelligence Sergeant:	Sergeant (E7).
Light Weapons Leader:	Sergeant (E7).
Medical Specialist:	Sergeant (E7).
Radio Supervisor:	Sergeant (E7).
Engineer Sergeant:	Sergeant (E7).
Assistant Medical Specialist:	Sergeant (E6).
Chief of Research and Development:	Sergeant (E5).
Engineer:	Sergeant (E5).

NOTE:
In the US Army ranks are grade from E1 (the lowest) upwards. E5 to E8 are grades within the rank of sergeant (British equivalents would be approximately: E5/6 = corporal; E7 = sergeant; E8 = staff-sergeant).

SFG(A) was deployed to Saudi Arabia as part III US Army and fought inside Kuwait and Iraq from the beginning of Operation *Desert Storm* in 1991.

● **7th Special Forces Group (Airborne)**
Operating in Central and South America, the 7th SFG(A) supported the *Contras* in Nicaragua and trained government forces in Honduras and El Salvador. One battalion of this group is based in Panama.

● **10th Special Forces Group (Airborne)**

Above: Special Forces "A Team" coming ashore on a training exercise. The main role of the Special Forces is the development of resistance behind enemy lines and a 12-man "A Team" is capable of organising, equipping and training a battalion-size guerrilla force of 650 men.

Until recently, this unit was intended to raid the Soviet lines of communication in Eastern Europe if the Warsaw Pact had ever attacked ▶

NATO. Its secondary operational theatre was Africa and the 10th SFG(A) has worked in Egypt, Sudan and southern African nations.

●Special Operations Aviation Brigade

This co-ordinates air support for the Special Forces and operates AH-6s, MH-6s, OH-6s, MH-60s and MH-47s. It also works closely with the Rangers: one AH-6 was lost over Panama, supporting the assault which Rio Hato. In 1987 the existence of a "black" (i.e. clandestine) unit known as *Task Force 160* was disclosed as Army helicopters attacked an Iranian minelaying vessel in the Persian Gulf. This is the 160th Aviation Battalion which includes AH-1 Cobra gunships as well as MH-60s and MH-47s for Special Forces airmobile assaults. Helicopters from the 160th flew members of 5th SFG(A) into Iraq

to monitor enemy troop movements, attack strategic targets and call in air strikes. There were several classic "hot" extractions when Iraqi forces located small patrols from 5th SFG(A): one eight-man recon team only escaped after a six-hour gun battle and repeated airstrikes left over 100 enemy dead.

●"Black" units

The Special Forces include secret formations which surface from time to time but whose work remains cloaked in mystery. These have included "Seaspray" — a joint Army/CIA unit formed in 1981 to transport Special Forces troops, primarily *Delta Force*, around the world; Intelligence Support Activity (ISA) and "Yellow Fruit"/Quick Reaction Team. The latter was reportedly tasked with anti-spetsnaz operations and operated under the guise of a phony commercial

company — *'Business Security International'*. It was closed down in the mid-1980s amid allegations of corrupt financial management.

Selection and training

Green Berets are "triple volunteers": they have volunteered for the Army, volunteered for Airborne training and are now volunteering for Special Forces. Training begins at Fort Bragg and consists of three phases:

Phase I teaches the basic skills of Special Forces work concentrating on patrolling, survival, navigation and physical endurance. The Green Beret is awarded to all those candidates who pass this stage.

Phase II includes methods of instruction, combat engineering, the use of foreign weapons, and specialist tasks like medical and communications training. The combat medic course is particularly testing since Green Berets will have to look after themselves — and provide essential medical care for foreign peoples.

Phase III puts the theory into practice, culminating in a guerrilla war exercise in North Carolina's Uwharrie National Forest where the trainee teams have to lead the local resistance. Citizens of Candor, North Carolina, take an active part in the training programme, playing the people and guerrillas of *"Pineland"* in a highly realistic exercise run by soldiers who have done all this for real in combat.

Below: Green Berets "A Team" speeding towards their objective on board a River Patrol Boat (PBR). These water-jet craft have a speed of 24 knots and were widely used in the Vietnam War; some 500 were built.

Above: The Green Berets have long made use of non-standard weapons to suit particular requirements; for example, the Uzi sub machine-gun.

▶ **Weapons and equipment**
In addition to standard US Army infantry weapons, the Special Forces have always employed those of their

Below: Applying camouflage greasepaint, the results of which will enable the wearer to blend into the background.

potential enemies or "non-attributable" weapons when behind the lines. These have ranged from Carl Gustav, Madsen and even ex-Wehrmacht MP40 sub-machine guns used in Vietnam, to Soviet and Chinese weapons. The now-discontinued Steyr GB 9mm pistol was popular during the 1980s since it is very tolerant of poor quality ammunition — which might be all the Green Berets can get once deployed far behind the lines. The Special Forces have had many weapons developed specifically for

them e.g. the High Standard .22 pistol with an integral silencer.

Uniform

Within the Special Forces there is a wide range of distinctive unit insignia including beret flashes and shoulder patches. The former were developed by General Yarborough in 1961 and are worn above the left eye. Enlisted men wear their unit crest on the flash; officers wear their rank insignia. Since 1984, non-Special Forces qualified personnel attached to the Special Forces have

Above: Learning to work with the minimum of back-up deep in the field is vital if a Special Forces mission is to remain undetected.

been authorised to wear the green beret and full SF insignia — an unpopular decision with the men who have earned it the hard way.

Below: Mission accomplished: an enemy target is destroyed deep in the jungle as a successful conclusion to another mission.

82nd Airborne Division

The paratroopers of the United States' 82nd Airborne Division were among the first soldiers to rush to the defence of Saudi Arabia in August 1990. Saddam Hussein seemed poised to continue his war of conquest; the 82nd, as America's rapid response force, was ordered to stop him. The Division has seen active service many times in the last 25 years: it was deployed in the Dominican Republic in 1965 and fought in Vietnam during 1968/69. In 1983, the 82nd played a key role in the invasion of Grenada and at the end of 1989 several of its battalions conducted an airborne assault on Panama.

The 82nd Infantry Division was originally raised in August 1917 at Camp Gordon, Georgia. Since the men mustered there hailed from every one of the 48 States, the new formation became known as the *All American* — the name stuck and the "AA" flash has since been worn with pride on battlefields from France to Indo-China. The 82nd was de-activated after World War I but re-activated in March 1942 after America found itself at war with Japan and Germany. Five

Below: Well protected against the elements during Operation *Desert Storm*, 82nd Airborne Division paratroopers wait to board one of their Blackhawks.

months later, the War Department ordered the 82nd to begin training as paratroops, with half of the personnel hived off to form the nucleus of the 101st Airborne. America's new airborne force subsequently took part in paratroop assaults in Sicily, Italy, Normandy and the Netherlands.

The role of the 82nd Airborne remains the same as it was during World War II: to seize important objectives by surprise parachute landings, and to hold them until slower, ground forces can link-up and relieve them. During the late-1970s, when the 82nd became part of the newly-formed Rapid Deployment Force, US strategy anticipated an air assault into Iran to forestall a Soviet invasion. The paratroopers would be grossly outnumbered and likely to be overwhelmed; hopefully they would buy time for US ground troops to be deployed. Very long range parachute landings were conducted, flying direct from the USA to Egypt during the Exercise *Bright Star* operations of the early-1980s. US-based paratroops were also dropped over Germany as part of NATO exercises, although the combat value of soldiers who jump after a 10-hour flight was obviously somewhat reduced.

The standard transport aircraft of the 82nd is the Lockheed C-141B Starlifter which can drop 168 fully-equipped paratroopers. Mass drops are frequently practised at night — like the Soviets, the American airborne forces recognise the futility of a daylight landing against ▶

Above: US Army paratrooper has his equipment checked prior to making a jump on Exercise *Bright Star '83*. Main parachute is on his back, reserve in front.

Above right: Men of the 82nd Airborne Division moving off from Salines Airfield, Grenada. This successful undertaking has raised morale in all US forces.

prepared opposition. They jump low enough to take ground fire: during the Panama attack, the first soldier in the doorway of a C-141B was killed before he could jump and the rest of the stick had to clamber past his body to get into action.

Organisation
The Division consists of three paratroop brigades; the 3/73rd Armor Battalion (43 x M551 Sheridan light tanks); and an aviation brigade of some 100 AH-64A Apache, OH-58 Kiowa and UH-60A Blackhawk helicopters. Immediate artillery support is provided by nine six-gun batteries of M101 105mm howitzers. Under the US Army's 1991 re-organisation, the Rapid Reaction Force will consist of the 82nd Airborne Division plus the 1st Cavalry, 7th and 24th Infantry and 101st Air Assault Divisions. All except the 7th Infantry Divison were deployed with the 82nd to Saudi Arabia to form the US XVIII Airborne Corps in 1990.

Selection and training
Every member of this volunteer unit,

including the 82nd's 250+ female soldiers, must maintain their jump status regardless of their role. The training process is predictably arduous, but results in a rather different calibre of soldier than the popular image. The "typical" paratrooper is about 24-years-old and some 40 per cent are married. Many take university courses in their own free time.

Weapons and equipment
Individual paratroopers jump with a T-10B parachute, a reserve 'chute, an M16A2 rifle and a 55lb (25kg) rucksack. Weighed down with allsorts of extras — ammunition for the machine-gun teams or mortars — they are still lightly equipped by comparison with the sort of mechanised infantry forces they must be prepared to fight. The greatest threat to airborne forces during World War II was enemy ▶

Right: Supreme fitness pays off in the desert for this member of a three-man 82nd AD mortar team, as he lugs the weapon's bulky baseplate.

armour: without a plentiful supply of anti-tank weapons, lightly equipped paratroops cannot resist a full-scale counter-attack. The 82nd Airborne has a formidable anti-tank capability with over 150 TOW missile launchers. With a maximum range of 12,300ft (3,750m) and a warhead capable of penetrating almost any main battle tank's frontal armour, TOW is the most effective missile of its kind in service.

The 82nd Airborne's 3rd Battalion, 73rd Armored Regiment is the only US combat unit to retain the M551 Sheridan light tank. This 18-ton aluminium vehicle is air-landed on a pallet while the crew parachute separately. It is armed with the controversial 152mm *Shillelagh* gun/missile system that fires a guided missile to a maximum range of over 13,100ft (4,000m). However, it has a minimum range of 3,300ft (1,000m) and uses a conventional anti-tank round to cover this "gap". Unfortunately, the savage recoil of this massive gun slews the turret around with enough force to break the gunner's wrist if he forgets to take his hand off the traversing wheel. The whole tank rocks backwards and the laser rangefinder is knocked out of alignment. The M551 has been replaced in the army reconnaissance squadrons originally issued with it, and it only soldiers on with the 82nd in the absence of any suitable replacement.

Uniform

The paratroopers wear standard US Army camouflage uniforms and the kevlar "Fritz" helmet. A newcomer to the Division earns his silver parachute wings and the right to wear a red beret after five jumps. The red, white, and blue "AA" badge was worn in Vietnam but has now been replaced on combat uniforms by subdued insignia — black over olive green.

Left: Although the Lockheed C-141B Starlifter acts as the 82nd AD's strategic air transport, the C-130 Hercules is used for air drops of a more tactical nature, as illustrated in this *Bright Star '83* drop conducted over the Egyptian desert.

75th Ranger Regiment

The 75th Ranger Regiment was created in April 1987, bringing together the three battalions of the 75th Infantry created since 1974. The new Ranger Regiment was presented with the lineage and honours won by Ranger battalions during World War II and the Korean War. The Ranger's history began before that of the United States: the first Ranger forces were irregular soldiers who fought during the French and Indian wars of the 18th Century. The most famous was known as *Roger's Rangers* after the unit's commander, but it was disbanded in 1763 at the end of the Seven Years War. This was an unfortunate precedent: throughout the 20th Century, the US Army has created Ranger battalions during wartime and abolished them shortly afterwards — only to find that it needed them again for the next conflict. The hard-won experience of the Ranger battalions of World War II was lost as the elite light infantry forces created from 1942 onwards were de-activated after 1945. Fresh Ranger units were created for the Korean War, only to suffer the same fate; and the same happened again during the Vietnam War.

The modern Rangers were assembled in the wake of the 1973 Arab-Israeli War. Israel survived the war largely thanks to an eleventh hour shipment of anti-tank missiles and other key weapons, rushed to Ben Gurion Airport by US aircraft. The US Army recognised that full-scale military intervention was a possibility in the future; and that for rapid deployment to the Middle East or to other strategic areas, it needed a special operations force. Such a unit had to be capable of everything from battalion-sized airborne assaults to raiding behind enemy lines: in other words, an elite light infantry formation similar to the Rangers of World War II. The 1st Battalion (Ranger) 75th Infantry was activated at Fort Benning in January 1974 and the 2nd Battalion was activated in October at Fort Lewis, Washington.

The Rangers were scheduled to have taken part in the Teheran hostage mission, flying into Iran to seize Manzarieh airfield from which the C-141 Starlifter transports would evacuate the hostages. Instead, their first operational deployment came in 1982 when the two battalions took part in the liberation of Grenada. Their action there was considered so successful that a third battalion was raised at Fort Benning during October 1984.

The Rangers played an important

Below: US Army Rangers of 75th Ranger Regiment on patrol in swamp country. They are armed with the M16A1 rifle; note how the nearest soldier has two magazines taped together to give rapid change-over in action.

role in Operation *Just Cause*, the invasion of Panama in December 1989. One Ranger battalion parachuted into Torrijos airport with elements of the 82nd Airborne Division. Another Ranger battalion jumped into Rio Hato, where the Panamanian dictator's most loyal troops were stationed. After a fierce gun battle, the Rangers seized the armoury there.

Organisation

The 75th Ranger Regiment consists of three battalions, each comprising three rifle companies and an HQ company. Total strength is about 2,000 men including the Regimental Recon Team which conducts amphibious operations as well as High-Altitude, Low Opening (HALO) and High-Altitude, High Opening (HAHO) parachute jumps.

Weapons and equipment

The Rangers use the standard small arms of the US Army: the rifle companies use M16A2 rifles, M249 Squad Automatic Weapons and M60 general purpose machine guns. The 90mm Recoilless Rifle (RR) has

Above: Ranger carrying M16A1 rifle fitted with M203 grenade launcher below the barrel. Sight for firing the grenade is above barrel. Range 1,310ft (400m).

been officially replaced by the new AT-4 RR although the Rangers continued to use the old weapon on exercises throughout the late-1980s, mainly firing canister rounds rather than the obsolete anti-tank projectile.

Selection and training

The severe 70-day course that leads to a "Ranger" qualification is not only for personnel volunteering for the Regiment. It is undertaken by many US officers and enthusiastic NCOs from other units who return to pass on their newly-learned skills. The course teaches tactical leadership and infantry skills under intense pressure: students get little sleep and are opposed on their exercises by very experienced "Aggressor" forces. At least one student in three fails to pass. The course consists of:
3d Ranger Company
Introductory phase teaching basic ▶

▶ infantry skills, unarmed combat and endurance — this weeds out quitters and culminates in students eading their first patrol.

2d Ranger Company
Combat patrolling in the forested mountains of Georgia with the emphasis on mountain warfare skills. This is followed by the desert warfare phase (introduced in 1983) which involves live-firing exercises conducted in Utah.

3d Ranger Company
L ve-firing, airmobile and small boat

exercises in the Florida swamps.

Uniforms

The Rangers wear standard US Army combat uniforms, distin-guished by Ranger patches. The 1st and 2nd Battalions raised in 1974 were supposed to wear a version of the patch worn by *Merrill's Marauders* in World War II, but they refused to adopt it. In its place they wore the traditional Ranger scroll of the type worn in Korea and Vietnam. This was officially

Rescue in Grenada October 25 1983

Following the inglorious end of the Vietnam War, American forces tried to keep a low profile on the international scene. Two rescue operations were attempted in efforts to secure the release of the crew of the *Mayaguez* and the Iranian embassy hostages. US troops also took part in various peacekeeping forces such as those

in the Sinai and in Beirut. However, major use of force was eschewed for both international and domestic reasons.

But in October 1983 President Reagan decided that the United States should join with six Carib-bean states in the invasion of the island of Grenada "to restore peace, order and respect for human rights;

recognised after their battalions' fine performance in Grenada. All three battalions now wear insignia similar to that of the 1st, 2nd and 3rd Ranger Battalions of World War II.

Right: The standard disruptive pattern combat uniform worn by this Ranger is augmented by the subdued greasepaint colours he has applied to his face. In the thick, dense forest, such camouflage techniques will help him blend into the background.

to evacuate those who wish to leave; and to help the Grenadians re-establish governmental institutions." On October 19, Grenada's Prime Minister, Maurice Bishop and several Cabinet members and labour leaders had been murdered by their former military associates, and a Revolutionary Military Council had later been announced, amid

Left: Grenada is a tiny island in the Caribbean but the USA was determined that it would not be another Cuba.

Below: US Rangers move off from Port Salines airfield, Grenada. It was a short, sharp campaign, lasting from October 25 to November 2, 1983, during which surprise played a major part in its undoubted success.

rumours that other government members had been murdered. US Intelligence reported Soviet/Cuban backing for the revolutionary regime, with Cubans actually establishing on the island new fortifications, arms caches and military communications.

President Regan viewed Grenada as "a Soviet-Cuban colony being readied as a major military bastion to export and undermine democracy." Uppermost in his mind was the position of some 1,000 US citizens, and especially the 600-odd young Americans at a medical school near the Port Salines airfield. The prospect of these youngsters being held hostage by the Marxist government was very serious and would have provided a far worse crisis than even that of the Iranian embassy staff. ▶

▶ Information on the resisting troops and their dispositions in Grenada seem to have been fairly sparse, but the US forces had three immediate objectives within the overall mission of the total capture of the whole island and the restoration of a democratic government. These three tasks were the freeing of the 600 medical students, the release of the governor (Sir Paul Scoones) and the defeat of the Cuban troops on the island. US Navy Seals were responsible for capturing the governor's residence, and Marines for the Pearls Airport on the island's east coast. The crucial task was, however, the taking of Port Salines airfield, which was being constructed and guarded by Cubans. This task was given to the Rangers.

Execution

The Marine assault on Pearls Airport began at 0500 hours (local) on October 25, while H-hour for the Rangers was 0536. The Rangers left the staging airfield on Barbados in the early hours aboard MC-130E Hercules aircraft of 8th Special Operations Squadron, 1st Special Operations Wing, USAF, based at Hurlburt Field in Florida. These aircraft were accompanied by AC-130 Hercules gunships (the famous "Spectres" of the Vietnam war) of 16th Special Operations Squadron.

As they came in over Port Salines searchlights were suddenly switched on, which quickly found the lumbering C-130s and enabled the anti-aircraft guns to open up on both the aircraft and the descending parachutists. The AC-130s were quickly called into action and silenced most of the Cuban guns. Among the lead elements in the assault was a 12-man team from the 317th Tactical Airlift Wing responsible for combat control of the drop, and these were quickly inside the air traffic control building.

Once on the ground the Rangers, told to expect some 500 Cubans (350 "workers" and a "small" military advisory team) found themselves under attack from some 600 well armed professional soldiers. The Cubans were armed with mortars and machine-guns, and had at least six armoured personnel carriers. A brisk battle developed in which the Rangers quickly gained the upper hand, and

Right: Men of 2/75th Rangers receive the Combat Infantry badge on return from Grenada.

Below: The US DoD released this photo to show the Soviet influence on Grenada.

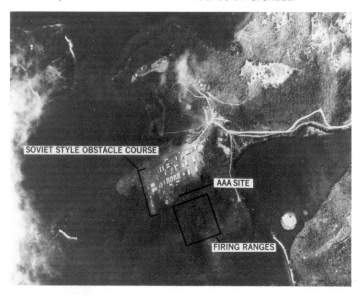

SOVIET STYLE OBSTACLE COURSE

AAA SITE

FIRING RANGES

by 0700 they were in complete control. The runway was cleared of obstacles (boulders, vehicles, pipes) and at 0715 the first C-130 of the second wave was able to land with reinforcements.

The Rangers then moved out, heading for the medical campus; brushing aside snipers and scattered resistance, they reached their objective by 0830 hours, to be greeted by some very relieved students. This campus — the True Blue medical college — was secured by 0850, although the other medical school at Grand Anse was not liberated until the following day by airborne troops.

Assessment

which ranger battalion took part has still not been announced publicly, although, in view of the haste.

with which the operation was mounted, it would seem that only the 1/75 in nearby Georgia could have reached the Caribbean in time. The Rangers played their part very wll. They led the assault on the airfield, against considerable resistance, secured their initial objective and went on to achieve the second all in just under 3½ hours. In fact, the whole Grenada operation was mounted so swiftly that no national or international opposition could be mobilised to resist it, and the actual attack, even though it took longer than anticipated, was over before anything more dangerous than words could be aimed at President Reagan and the US Administration. It was a real military success, and one in which the Rangers acquitted themselves well, as usual.

Delta Force

US Army Colonel Charles Beckwith served with the British SAS in 1962-63 and on his return to the US Army sought to form a unit with the same organisation, ideals and functions as the SAS. After numerous attempts spread over many years he succeeded, and the new force — named 1st Special Forces Operational Detachment-Delta (Delta, for short) — was authorised on November 19, 1977. This unit should not be confused with the Delta Project (Detachment B-52) set up by the Special Forces in Vietnam in the mid-1960s (and at one time commanded by Beckwith), which was a totally different organsiation and concept.

The prime role of Delta was to deal with terrorist incidents affecting US interests, a very topical requirement in the light of the rash of such incidents at that time, such as the Munich Olympic Games hostage incident (August 1972) and the Mogadishu rescue operation by GSG 9 (October 1977).

Following its setting up, Delta proceeded to select and train its men, and various unit tasks were successfully undertaken. Then, on November 4, 1979, Iranian "students" broke into the US Embassy in Teheran, taking all the staff hostage, and from then on Delta was increasingly deeply involved in planning a rescue operation, culminating in the actual attempt on April 24/25, 1980.

Organisation

Following the SAS pattern, Delta itself is divided into squadrons, which in turn are sub-divided into troops. The troops are 16 men strong, capable of operating either as a troop, or in two groups of eight, four groups of four, or eight groups of two. In its early stages there was only one squadron (A Squadron) but this split into two, forming B Squadron, in early 1979.

The debacle in Iran led to a great deal of soul-searching within the US

Left: Lightweight, small and very "high-tech", this mini satellite receiver dish is a fine example of the sort of state-of-the-art technology used by *Delta Force* during Operation *Desert Storm*. Note the carrying case.

Above: As with the majority of elite units, *Delta Force* trains on foreign-made arms, such as this Czech-built 7.62mm Model 58P rifle. Such weapons can subsequently be used for deception purposes.

Special Forces. Yet the primary reasons for the failure were not attributable to Colonel Beckwith and *Delta Force*. On the technical side, the decision to use US Navy Sikorsky RH-53 helicopters instead of the more appropriate HH-53s was necessary because of the Soviet threat. The tail booms of an RH-53 can be folded, allowing the helicopter to be taken below decks; HH-53s do not have this facility. The Soviets were watching USS *Nimitz* from the air and with satellites — the sight of eight large helicopters on the flight deck might well have led a shrewd Soviet observer to guess what was coming — and they *may* have alerted the Iranians. Other technical difficulties with this long-range operation were compounded by President Carter's administration which was determined to micro-manage the entire mission from Washington, DC.

Delta Force was back in the desert ten years later, spearheading the US Special Forces raids inside Iraq. Saddam Hussein had many more SS-1 "Scud" missiles than western intelligence agencies had credited him with and the continued rain of missiles on Israel could not be allowed to continue. Israel's Prime Minister Shamir threatened retaliation in kind — and Israel secretly fired a nuclear-capable (but inert) ballistic missile into the Mediterranean as a final warning. General Carl Stiner, C-in-C. Special Operations Command, and Major-General Wayne A. Downing, Commander of the Joint Special Operations Command told the Joint Chiefs of Staff that their elite teams could find many more "Scuds" than the satellites.

Delta Force soldiers flew into Iraq as part of a joint operation that involved elements of the British SAS. Operating from MH-53J "Pave Low III" helicopters of the 20th SOS they tracked down Saddam's missiles and targeted them for air strikes. On 27 February 1991, the final day of the ground war, *Delta Force* discovered a battery of 26 "Scuds" being readied for a final barrage on Israel. They were summarily destroyed. General Schwarz-

Right: A *Delta Force* trooper involved in Operation *Eagle Claw*, as the mission comes to a fiery end at Desert One. A patch covering a US flag on his jacket would have been ripped off at the US Embassy.

Below: As the sun sets over the sea, one of the ill-fated Sikorsky RH-53D Sea Stallion helicopters involved in the attempt to rescue US hostages in Iran lifts off from the deck of USS *Nimitz*.

US Navy watchkeeping woollen knitted cap

M60 7.62mm MG

US flag recognition patch covered with black tape

Belted 7.62mm ammunition

Grenade

Water bottle

Levis

Unpolished black leather boots

139

kopf sent a personal message of congratulation, thanking the team for keeping Israel out of the war. The mission was accomplished at the cost of three *Delta Force* soldiers; Patrick Hurley, Otto Clark and Eloy Rodriguez Jr. who died when the Sikorsky UH-60 Black-hawk transport helicopter they were flying in crashed into a sand dune.

Selection and Training

Delta Force remains dedicated to anti-terrorist duties despite its work in the Gulf War. At Fort Bragg, North Carolina, it has an extensive training area which includes a Boeing 727 aircraft used to practice hostage-rescue assaults. There is also the famous Close Quarter Battle House — better known as the "Haunted

Operation Eagle Claw Rescue attempt in Iran, 1980

On November 4, 1979 a group of Iranian "students" poured into the US Embassy compound in Teheran and held the 53 occupants hostage for the ensuing months, plus a further three in the Foreign Ministry. From the earliest days of the crisis one of the options under constant review and development was a military rescue, although both diplomatic and military endeavours were constantly bedevilled by the continuing chaos in Iran, the uncertain ever-changing intentions of the captors, and the vacillating position of the Iranian leadership. An unchanging factor was the remoteness of Teheran from available US bases. The plan that was eventually decided upon centred on Colonel Beckwith and Delta, although it obviously involved many more both directly and indirectly. The overall codename was Operation Eagle Claw, while the helicopter element was designated Operation Evening Light.

The plan

The plan was relatively simple, complicated mainly by the problems of time and space, and comprised some preliminary moves and a three-phase operation.
Preliminary moves. In the preliminary moves Delta was to fly, via Germany and Egypt, to Masirah airfield in Oman. There they would transfer to C-130s and, flying at very low level to avoid the radar, cross the Gulf of Oman and southern Iran to land at Desert One, a remote site in the Dasht-e-Karir Salt Desert, 265 nautical miles (490km) south east of Teheran. Meanwhile, eight US Navy RH-53D helicopters, which had

been deployed some weeks earlier via Diego Garcia would take off from the USS *Nimitz* and, flown (also at very low level) by their US Marine Corps crews, join up with the main party at Desert One.
Phase I: Insertion. At Desert One the plan was for the six C-130s (three troop carriers; three to refuel the helicopters) to land and await the helicopters, who were scheduled to arrive some 30 minutes later. Because Desert One was beside a road (judged to be little used) a 12-strong Road Watch Team was the first to deploy to intercept and detain any passing Iranians. When they had refuelled the helicopters were to load the assault team and fly on towards Teheran, dropping off the men at a landing-zone and then proceeding to their helicopter hide some 15 miles (24km) to the north. The assault group was to be met by two agents at the landing zone and guided by them to a remote wadi, some 5 miles away (8km). Helicopters and men would then rest in their hides through the day.
Phase IIA: The rescue. After last light one agent would take the 12 drivers/translators to collect six Mercedes trucks, while the other agent would take Colonel Beckwith on a route reconnaissance. At 2030 hours the complete unit would embus at the hide and drive to Teheran, the actual rescue operation starting between 2300 and 2400 hours. Having disposed of the guards and released the hostages, it was planned to call in the helicopters, either to the embassy compound if an LZ could be cleared (the students had erected poles to prevent a surprise landing)

House". *Delta Force* maintains two 100-man squadrons ready for action but has many more personnel devoted to training other special warfare units in anti-terrorist or counter-insurgency roles.

Weapons and Equipment

Delta Force has access to any weapons it needs. Primary anti-terrorist weapons include SIG-Sauer 9mm pistols (adopted in 1990 by the British SAS); Heckler and Koch MP5 sub machine-guns; and the full range of US Army small arms and other specialist firearms, like the Barrett and McMillan .50in calibre sniper rifles and the folding-stock para version of FN's M249 Squad Automatic Weapon.

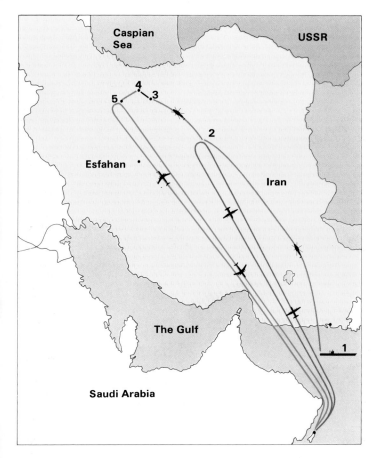

or, if this was impracticable, to a nearby football stadium. Once all the hostages were clear the assault party would be taken out by helicopter, the White Element (see table) being the last out.

Phase IIB: Rescue at the Foreign Ministry. Concurrently with Phase IIA the 13-man special team would assault the Foreign Ministry, rescue ▶

Above: The Eagle Claw plan was for helicopters (red) to fly from USS *Nimitz* (1) to Desert One (2), pick up Delta, flown in by C-130 (blue), then fly to hides (3) near Teheran (4). Helicopters would take the freed hostages to an airstrip (5) held by US Rangers. They would then fly out in C-141s (green).

▶ the hostages there, and take them to an adjacent park where they would all be picked up by a helicopter.

Phase III: Extraction. While the action was taking place in Teheran a Ranger contingent would seize Manzarieh airfield, some 35 miles (56km) to the south, and several C-141 turbojet transports would fly in. Once everyone had been evacuated from Teheran to Manzarieh they would be flown out in the C-141s, the Rangers leaving last. All surviving helicopters would be abandoned at Manzarieh.

Contingency plans. Various contingencies were foreseen and plans made accordingly; for example, in the event that not enough helicopters were available to lift everyone out of Teheran in one lift. One critically important condition had been agreed throughout the planning, namely that there had to be an absolute minimum of six helicopters to fly out of Desert One.

Command and control. The ground force commander was Colonel Beckwith, who reported to Major-General James Vaught, the Commander Joint Task Force (COMJTF) who was at Wadi Kena airfield in Egypt; they were linked by portable satellite systems. General Vaught had a similar link back to Washington, DC, where General David Jones, the Chairman of the Joint Chiefs of Staff, was in session with President Jimmy Carter throughout

the critical hours of the operation. In a last-minute change of plans Air Force Colonel James Kyle was appointed commander at Desert One.

Operation Eagle Claw: Ground Personnel

Group	Strength	Origin	Task
Main Assault Group:			Secure Western end of compound.
Red Element	40		Secure Eastern sector of Embassy.
Blue Element	40	Delta	Secure Roosevelt Avenue during
White Element	13		main action, then cover withdrawal to football stadium.
Foreign Ministry Assault Team	13	Special Forces unit	Rescue 3 hostages held in Foreign Ministry building in Teheran.
Road Watch Team	12	Rangers	Mostly Rangers, but with some Delta soldiers.
Driving Team	12	Volunteers	6 drivers; 6 assistants/interpreters.
Iranian general	2	—	General on-site assistance
DoD Agents	4	—	Positioned in Teheran prior to operation; organise/act as guides.
Manzarieh Airfield Defence Team	Company	Rangers	Take and hold airfield for fly-out.
Commander Joint Task Force (COMJTF)	?	?	Located at Wadi Kena, Egypt, then fly to Manzarieh during evacuation phase.

Execution

The C-141 airlift of the ground party from the USA to Masirah went according to plan, as did the C-130 flights to Desert One. The ▶

Above: RH-53Ds are readied for Eagle Claw. Optimised for minesweeping, the RH-53D had good range and payload and was shipboard compatible.

Operation Eagle Claw: Aircraft

Aircraft	Type	Number	Tasks
MC-130E Hercules	Special operations aircraft with special avionics fit.	3	Fly men and stores from Masirah to Desert One. Two to return to Masirah at once (empty), the third to wait for Road Watch Team.
EC-130E Hercules	Command and control conversion of C-130	3	Carry fuel from Masirah to Desert One to refuel helicopters.
RH-53D Sea Stallion	Minesweeping version of H-53 helicopter, selected because of its combination of range, payload, shipboard compatibility and security considerations.	8	Fly empty from USS *Nimitz* to Desert One. Pick up men, fly them to hide site, then go to separate helicopter hide. Next night fly to Teheran, extract hostages/rescue force and take to Mansarieh.
AC-130E Hercules	Specialised "gunship" version of C-130.	4	One over Teheran to prevent Iranian reinforcements reaching embassy. One over Teheran airfield to prevent Iranian aircraft taking off. Two reserves.
C-141 Starlifter	Military transport aircraft	3	Fly into Manzarieh to extract whole force on completion of operation.
C-130 Hercules	Military tactical transport	3(?)	Fly Ranger company into Manzarieh to take and hold airfield.

▶ first aircraft, carrying Colonels Beckwith and Kyle, Blue Element and the Road Watch Team, landed safely and the Road Watch Team deployed, immediately having to stop a bus containing 45 people who were detained under guard. Minutes later two more vehicles appeared from the south; the first, a petrol tanker, was hit by an anti-tank rocket and burst into flames, but the driver escaped in the second vehicle which drove off at high speed. The first C-130 then took off, leaving those on the ground briefly on their own. The second C-130 then came in and unloaded and, after the remaining four C-130s had landed, took off again for Masirah. The four C-130s and the ground party then waited for the helicopters—and waited.

The helicopters were, quite literally, the key to the operation. The eight helicopters had taken off from USS Nimitz (some 50 miles off the Iranian coast) at 1930 hours (local) and headed north for Desert One. At about 2145 hours helicopter No 6 indicated an impending catastrophic blade failure, one of the two really critical problems requiring an abort. The crew landed, confirmed the prob-

lem, removed sensitive documents and were then picked up by helicopter No 8 which then followed the other some minutes behind.

About one hour later the leading RH-53Ds ran into a very severe and totally unexpected dust storm; all emerged from this, flew on for an hour and then encountered a second and even worse dust storm. The helicopter force commander—Major Seiffert, USMC—had earlier lost his inertial navigation system and, entirely blinded, flew back out of the first dust storm and landed, accompanied by helicopter No. 2. Major Seiffert had a secure radio link to COMJTF, who told him that the weather at Desert One was clear; consequently, after some 20 minutes on the ground both aircraft took off again and followed the others to Desert One.

Meanwhile, helicopter No. 5 suffered a major electrical failure and lost most instruments. With no artificial horizon or heading, and with mountains ahead, he was compelled to abort, and returned to the Nimitz: thus leaving six helicopters to continue the mission.

The first helicopter (No. 3) cleared the dust storm some 30nm (56km) from Desert One and,

using the burning Iranian petrol tanker as a beacon, landed some 50 minutes late. The remaining aircraft straggled in over the next half-an-hour, all coming from different directions (except Nos. 1 and 2, which were together). The crews were very shaken by their experience, but the helicopters were quickly moved to their tanker C-130s, refuelling began, and the assault party started to board their designated aircraft.

Colonel Beckwith was fretting on the ground, 90 minutes behind schedule when he was informed that helicopter No. 2 had had a partial hydraulic failure during the flight; the pilot had continued to Desert One in the hope of effecting repairs, but these proved impossible. After a quick discussion, Colonel Kyle spoke to General Vaught in Egypt, who countered with a suggestion that they continue with five, despite the agreed plan that six was the absolute minimum.

The decision to call the whole thing off was quickly reached, however, although whether it was made at Desert One or in far-off Washington has never been clearly established. But there was no problem in aborting at this stage, the only minor complication being that helicopter No. 4, which had been on the ground longest, needed to top up with fuel before setting off to the *Nimitz*. Only one C-130 had enough fuel left and to clear a space for No. 4 helicopter No. 3 took off and banked to the left, but, because of the height (5,000ft/ 1,525m) and its weight (42,000lb/ 19,050kg), it could not maintain the hover and slid back straight into the C-130. It was just 0240 hours.

The effect was instantaneous and disastrous: both aircraft exploded, debris flew around and ammunition began to cook off. Five USAF aircrewmen in the C-130 and three marines in the RH-53D died, but 64 Delta men inside the C-130 escaped quickly from the aircraft and rescued the loadmaster. The decision was then made to abandon the remaining helicopters and the whole party returned to Masirah in the three C-130s.

Below: RH-53D helicopters flying in formation before the raid. They were both the key to success and the ultimate cause of the operation's failure.

Marine Corps

The United States Marine Corps (USMC) is the world's largest elite force. With a strength of some 194,000 men and women in three divisions and three air wings with 416 combat aircraft, it is even bigger then the total armed forces of most countries. Since it was raised by order of Congress on November 10, 1775, the USMC has taken part in every major war fought by the USA, as well as in numerous "police" actions and armed interventions all over the world. Its record is impressive and battles such as Belleau Wood, Guadalcanal, Iwo Jima, Chosin reservoir, and Khe Sanh have earned it a special place in military history.

The missions assigned to the USMC fall into three broad categories. The principal mission is to maintain an amphibious capability for use in conjunction with fleet operations, including the seizure and defence of advanced naval bases and the conduct of land operations essential to the successful execution of a maritime campaign. In addition, the Corps is required to provide security detachments for naval bases and the Navy's principal warships. Finally, the Corps carries out any addtional duties placed upon it by the President of the USA.

The Marine Corps deployed over half its strength to the Gulf during the conflict with Iraq. Over 72,000 Marines — two Divisions and two Air Wings — were ashore for the ground offensive in February, while some 18,000 Marines remained afloat, poised to attack the coast of Kuwait. Much-publicised marine amphibious exercises in the weeks before the Allied attack led the Iraqis to concentrate their forces around Kuwait City in expectation of a classic seaborne attack. Instead, the Allied armies swept around the open desert flank and cut off all Saddam Hissein's troops in occupied Kuwait. The Marines spearheaded the drive on Kuwait City and fought the biggest tank battle in the history of the Corps when they defeated Iraqi armoured brigades near Kuwait International Airport.

Organisation

Current active-duty strength of the USMC is some 194,000 (including 4,000 women), with some 38,000 reserves. These are organised into four divisions and four aircraft wings (three regular and one reserve of each), but both organisations are larger than their counterparts in the other services. This is particularly apparent in the division which, with a strength of 18,000 is some 20 per cent larger than a US Army division.

The USMC emphasises combined arms tactics and operate in Marine Air-Ground Task Forces: closely integrating their air support with all-arms battlegroups on the ground. Each division has three infantry regiments, each of three battalions, plus a reconnaissance battalion of 8 x 8 LAVs and attached M60A1 main battle tanks. Each rifle battalion has an HQ company, service company, weapons company and three rifle companies.

The standard Marine aircraft wing (MAW) has 18 to 21 squad-

Current USMC Deployment	
1st Marine Air Wing (Okinawa, Japan.)	Operates in support of 3rd Marine Expeditionary Force.
2nd Marine Air Wing (Cherry Point, NC.)	Operates in support of 2nd Marine Expeditionary Force.
3rd Marine Air Wing (El Toro, Ca.)	Operates in support of 1st Marine Expeditionary Force.
4th Marine Air Wing (New Orleans, La.)	Operates in support of Marine Reserve Forces.

rons equipped with between 286 and 315 fixed- and rotary-winged types ranging from fighter/attack (the F/A-18 Hornet), through medium attack (the A-6 Intruder and the AV-8 Harrier) and on to tanker/transport (KC-130 Hercules) and helicopter assets (AH-1 SeaCobra, CH-46 Sea Knight, the CH-53 Sea Stallion and UH-1 Huey). There are also support squadrons with OV-10 Broncos and EA-6B Prowlers.

Above: US Marine in standard combat uniform. Note the "flak" vest and canvas "jungleboots". There are some 194,000 men and women in the USMC, making it one of the largest elite forces, and bigger than the total armed forces of many nations. Training is tough and discipline severe. The USMC also has a very strong lobby in Congress and a good image with the US public.

▶ Weapons and equipment

The single dominant characteristic of Marine tactical doctrine is the emphasis on the principle of offensive action, which applies to all aspects of the Corps' activities. This ethos has a major effect on the way the USMC is equipped.

The Marines are equipped with AAV-7 amphibious assault vehicles: giant personnel carriers that can "swim" ashore in up to 10 feet (3m) of surf. Current tactical thinking stresses "vertical envelopment": landing Marines and LAVs by helicopter behind the enemy forces defending the beach. Hence the importance of AH-1T SeaCobra gunships with their 20mm cannon, rockets and TOW anti-tank missiles.

Infantry companies are armed with M16A2 rifles; M203 40mm grenade launchers; M249 Squad Automatic Weapons and M60E3 general-purpose machine-guns. The M60E3, adopted in 1985, is a lighter and better version of the old M60 used by the Army. Support weapons include 60mm light mortars and the Shoulder-fired Assault Weapon; a bazooka-like "bunker buster". Anti-tank weapons range from the M47 Dragon anti-tank guided missile, AT-4 and TOW. Marine artillery batteries are equipped with M198 155mm howitzers; M109 self-propelled howitzers and British 105mm light guns. The Marines' elderly M60A1 tanks appeared in the Gulf sporting "bricks" of reactive armour and new fire control systems: elements within the Corps are calling for these to be replaced by M1 Abrams tanks. ▶

Above right: M60A1 MBTs have been the mainstay of the USMC armoured force for many years and remain so today, albeit in modest numbers and with a limited fighting capability.

Right: USMC gunner using an M2 Browning 0.50in (12.7mm) heavy machine-gun mounted on top of a tank-landing craft to provide defensive fire.

Below: USMC reconnaissance group hurry ashore with their inflatable boat. Such recce groups would normally land under cover of darkness when on a covert mission.

▶ The USMC's standard attack fighter is the F/A-18 Hornet, which equips 13 active squadrons plus one in the Marine Corps Reserve. It is also to be found in use as a pilot trainer. The USMC was an early supporter of the V/STOL Harrier and now operates the AV-8B Harrier II model in the fighter/ground attack roles. There are now some 150 of these fighters in front-line service, and a further 30+ two-seater TAV-8A/Bs for use in the pilot training role.

Selection and training

All members of the US Armed Forces are now volunteers, and those for the USMC enlist direct into the Corps. Recruits go straight to one of the two training depots, at San Diego, Ca, and Parris Island, SC, where they undergo the famous 11-week "boot camp". This is an experience which all who undergo thoroughly appreciate once they have finished it, but that does not imply that anything would ever make them do it again!

Surprisingly, despite its size, the USMC does not have its own officer academy, although some are accepted from the Navy academy at Annapolis. The main source of officers is through the Naval ROTC, Officers Candidate School (OCS) or the Platoon Leaders Class. All officer candidates (including those from Annapolis) must undergo a rigorous selection and training course at Quantico, before being accepted for a full commission.

The Mayaguez Incident May 12 1975

On May 12, 1975 a US ship, the SS *Mayaguez*, was seized by Cambodian gunboats in the Gulf of Thailand, 6½ miles off the island of Poulo Wai. The radio operator managed to transmit a message for help. President Gerald Ford quickly authorised firm action and on May 14 a 230-strong USMC group was flown from Okinawa to the USAF base at U-Tapao in south-east Thailand, which was some 223 miles (359km) from Koh Tang Island. The marines' transport to the operational area was to be provided by 14 USAF helicopters: seven HH-53 (code Jolly Greens, JG) and seven CH-53 (code Knife, K), although not all were available at the start of the operation. Both types were armed and protected with armour plate, but only the Jolly Green version could be refuelled in flight.

The nearest US Navy ship was the frigate USS *Harold E Holt*, which was fortuitously in the area, with the frigate USS *Henry B Wilson* and the fleet carrier USS *Coral Sea* steaming at flank speed from the north east, heading for the scene of the action.

The US forces knew that the *Mayaguez* was anchored 1½ miles (2.4km) north of Koh Tang island, but the whereabouts of the crew was uncertain. The plan was, therefore, somewhat open-ended:

Three helicopters would take some marines to the USS *Holt* to form a boarding party to retake the *Mayaguez*.

Eight helicopters would land a first-wave of marines at dawn on the northern beaches of Koh Tang to establish a base.

The second wave would then be flown to Koh Tang.

A third wave would be in reserve to exploit the tactical situation as it developed.

The battle

About 0645 (H-hour) two CH-53s —Knife 21 (K21) and K22—flew into West Beach, but as marines streamed over the lowered landing-ramp of K21 devastating fire was brought to bear at short range from enemy rifles, rockets and mortars. Surprise was total and one of K21's engines was damaged. Having offloaded its passengers, K21 flew off but had to be ditched a mile offshore. On the arrival of K32 and Jolly Green 41 (JG41), K22 headed back into the beach to land its marines; it was under fire the whole way in and suffered many hits, one of which caused a major fuel leak. Unable to land, K22 struggled to the mainland where it

USMC Airpower

Aircraft Type	Function	Squadrons
F/A-18 Hornet	Fighter/Attack	14 plus training
A-6 Intruder	Medium Attack	4 plus training
AV-8 Harrier II	Light Attack	8 plus training
AH-1 SeaCobra	Light Attack	*8
EA-6B Prowler	Electronic Warfare	1
EA-6A Intruder	Electronic Warfare	1
OV-10 Bronco	Observation	3
KC-130 Hercules	Tanker/Transport	4
CH-53 Sea Stallion	Heavy Transport	10
CH-46 Sea Knight	Medium Transport	17
UH-1 Iroquois	Light Transport	*6
F-5 Tiger II	Aggressor/DACT	1
C-9B Skytrain II	VIP Transport	1
UC-12B	Utility	Base Flights

*The AH-1s and UH-1s are operated in six composite squadrons. The Marine Corps Reserve also operates two AH-1 equipped units.
A single Marine Air Wing has more tactical airpower than most of the world's national air forces — and there are four MAWs.

---

made an emergency landing on the beach.

K32, fully loaded with passengers, dumped fuel before rescuing 3 of the 4 crew of the ditched K21 and then, accompanied by JG41, it flew to West Beach. Despite receiving 75 hits, including at least one from a rocket, K32 managed to land and offload its passengers, and then, with a

Below: May 15, 1975. A Marine and USAF pararescueman run to a USAF HH-53 helicopter during the Koh Tang operation. The refuelling capability was vital.

seriously wounded crewman, a wounded marine and the survivors of K21, returned to U-Tapao. JG41 was prevented from landing by the intense fire and eventually had to leave for an air-to-air refuelling from an HC-130P.

Events on East Beach followed a similar pattern, with K23 and K31 coming under heavy fire as they were about to touch down. K23 was hit in the rotor system and engines, and the pilot slammed it into the beach, ordering all 20 marines aboard to abandon the aircraft. K31 was also seriously damaged and the captain ditched ▶

▶ in the shallows; of the 26 on board 18 survived and escaped, but of these four were killed and one other died later. The survivors from K31 swam out to sea where all were subsequently rescued.

At sea the USS *Holt* had found the *Mayaguez*, but discovered that she was deserted. Thus, by H+1 hour the ship had been retaken (but without her crew), there were 25 men on East Beach (survivors from K23), 29 on West Beach, 13 were swimming out to sea, and of the 5 helicopters so far involved 3 had been destroyed, one ditched on the mainland and the fifth badly damaged.

Next to approach West Beach were JG42 and JG43 on their first run in, and JG41 returning from refuelling. JG41 was driven off with more hits, and then JG42 and JG43 were also forced back. JG43 flew down the coast and landed its 29 marines (including the CO) on a tiny LZ 875 yards (800m) to the south, although this proved of dubious value as they took many hours to fight their way back to join the main body. JG42, meanwhile, managed to land its marines on West Beach, but suffered heavy damage and had to return to U-Tapao escorted by JG43. JG41 then tried yet again to land its marines, but eventually had to go for yet another refuelling.

At about 0800 hours three more helicopters became available, but JG13 was immediately damaged trying to extract the 25 survivors of K23 from East Beach, and had to go back to U-Tapao. On West Beach JG41 had direct support from a C-130 Spectre gunship, including fire from a 105mm cannon. With this assistance the pilot brought JG41 in to land but came under mortar fire (including one bomb which passed through the rotor disc) and he flew off to refuel again with five passengers still aboard. He had been airborne for eight hours and was ordered back to base where his aircraft was grounded due to the extensive damage.

It was at this point that a local fishing boat returned the missing crew of the *Mayaguez* to the frigate

USS *Wilson*, having brought them from another island near the mainland. The Americans' aim then changed at once to retrieving the marines from Koh Tang, but this was easier said than done. The five remaining helicopters now approached Koh Tang with reinforcements. K52 tried to land but was hit repeatedly and her fuel tanks holed; since Knifes lacked an air-to-air refuelling capability the pilot had to return to the mainland.

On West Beach K51 and JG43, despite heavy fire, delivered their passengers, and K51 was even able to extract five badly wounded marines. JG43, still undamaged, met up with a circling HC-130P to take on yet more fuel. The second pair of helicopters (JG11, JG12) also succeeded in putting their marines ashore; JG12 took casualties aboard and departed for the mainland, while JG11 flew to the tanker, topped-up and returned at once to Koh Tang.

Meanwhile, the CO and his 29 men reached the West Beach main position, having fought hard all the way up, and with many captured weapons to prove it. Thus, at noon there were 222 men ashore, 197 on the West Beach, but with 25 still marooned on the East Beach. The larger force had managed to penetrate as far as a clearing half-way across the "Neck", but the Cambodians prevented any further progress. Another helicopter rescue was tried at about 1430 hours, following heavy bombardment and a CS gas attack (which failed due to contrary winds). JG43 was first in, but came under heavy fire and with heavy damage and several casualties was forced to limp off to the USS *Coral Sea*, by now some 70 miles (113km) away. JG11 then flew in, supported by fire from JG12, K51 and the USS *Wilson*'s long-boat armed with two MGs. All 25 USMC and USAF men (helicopter crew) on the beach were taken off and flown to the *Coral Sea* and the focus of attention shifted to West Beach.

With darkness falling K51 went in under fire and rescued a full load of

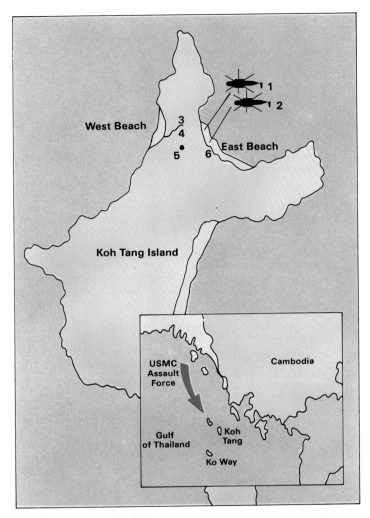

Above: The assault force was flown from Thailand. Two helicopters were shot down (1,2) and their crews pinned down (6).

Other landings on West Beach reached the clearings (3,4). AC-130 dropped a 15,000lb bomb (5) with no effect.

marines. JG43 then took on board 54 men, and both flew off to the *Coral Sea*. JG44 then went in, loaded up and took off, leaving 73 marines in a 50-yard (46m) perimeter on the beach, and under intense fire. JG44's pilot decided that the situation was so acute that he could save the 20 minute trip to the *Coral Sea* by landing his passengers on the USS *Holt*. With a crewman hanging out the door giving directions he got one main-

wheel on the corner of the flight-deck with only two feet (0.6m) of clearance for the rotor disc. He then returned to the beach, took off another load of marines but, due to engine power loss was forced to fly to the *Coral Sea*.

K51 returned quickly for the 29 marines remaining ashore. With 27 marines aboard a crewman had to run up the beach to grab the last two who were still giving covering fire at the jungle's edge.

SEALs

The Sea Air Land (SEAL) teams are America's elite amphibious operations forces and they command great respect among other special warfare units. A development of the old Underwater Demolition Teams, the SEALs are tasked with the covert reconnaissance of enemy-held coastline — particularly in advance of a possible US Marine Corps landing. Yet the SEALs responsibilities have grown to include all manner of special operations. In Vietnam they fought along the thousands of miles of waterways that make up the Mekong Delta; penetrating deep into communist-controlled territory, they raided Viet Cong bases and ambushed enemy patrols. Some SEAL teams were tasked with the recovery of American prisoners of war known to be held in remote jungle camps. They did track down several such camps and rescued

many captured South Vietnamese, but the Viet Cong always managed to spirit away their American PoW captives.

The SEALs' outstanding combat record in Vietnam saved them from the malaise that afflicted US Army special warfare forces after the withdrawal from South-East Asia. During the mid-1980s there were still 37 platoons of SEALs, all capable of independent operation, and the ▶

Right: A member of a US Navy Underwater Demolition Team (UDT). Dating from World War II, the UDTs have been replaced by SEAL teams.

Below: SEAL team on a beach reconnaissance in 1983. Nearest man is carrying the Stoner Mark 23 Commando MG, a weapon unique to the SEALs; a 5.56mm weapon, it is also known as M63.

number had risen to 50 by 1990. US Special Operations Command now plans to increase this to 60.

SEALs joined Army Special Forces and *Delta Force* to lead the invasion of Panama in 1989. The SEALs ran into bitter resistance while trying to disable President Noriega's intended getaway — a Lear Jet at Paitilla Airfield — and four SEALs were killed in action before the Panamanian troops were driven back and the target finally destroyed.

In the Gulf War, SEAL teams swam ashore all along the coast of Kuwait to spy on the Iraqi defences before the ground war began. The Iraqis never detected the presence of the SEALs whose reports convinced Allied commanders that an amphibious landing would be extremely hazardous — but it would be worthwhile convincing Saddam Hussein that the Marines would still attempt one. On the night of February 23/24 1991, six SEALs paddled ashore on the Kuwaiti coast and planted explosive charges before raking the Iraqi defences with machine-gun fire from their speedboats. The Iraqis fired blindly into the night, ducking as the beach rocked with a succession of explosions. While the SEALs made themselves scarce, the Iraqis rushed more troops to the coast to meet the landing that seemed to be underway; meanwhile Allied armoured forces began to break through Iraq's southern defensive line instead. It was a classic diversionary operation, illustrating perfectly how a handful of determined men can achieve results out of all proportion to their small numbers.

Organisation

The US Navy Special Operations Forces consist of: Naval Special Warfare Group 1 (NSWG 1), based at Coronado, California; and NSWG 2, based at Little Creek, Virginia. Each consists of two SEAL teams, plus three Special Boat Units, one SEAL Delivery Vehicle Team and a Light Attack helicopter squadron. In addition, there are Naval Special Warfare Units with varying numbers of SEAL platoons in Scotland, the Philippines and Portugal. Full details of deployment are obviously classified. A full SEAL team has 27 officers and 156 petty officers and seamen divided between five platoons. SEAL Team Six — the US Navy's anti-terrorist unit — is attached to *Delta Force* and comes under Joint Special Operations Command control.

Selection and training

SEAL training is astonishingly hard and over half the candidates who begin a course will fail to stay the distance. It requires mental toughness as much as sheer physical staying power; during the infamous "Hell Week" (Week 6 of the course) the students receive only 4 hours sleep in six days. The SEAL course involves all aspects of amphibious reconnaissance and raiding plus comprehensive training in High Altitude Low Opening and High Altitude High Opening parachute descent techniques.

Right: Members of a SEAL Delivery Vehicle Team on board a Swimmer Delivery Vehicle (SDV). The Team form part of NSWG 1 based in California.

Below: Deep-Sea Rescue Vehicle-1 (DSRV-1) on a low-loader. This 32 ton vessel is designed for rescue, but could well also have a combat capability with Special Warfare Units.

▶ Weapons and equipment

The SEALs' most common personal firearm is the Heckler and Koch MP5 9mm sub-machine gun. This is available in numerous versions ideal for specialist units. All manner of handguns are used since the SEALs are one of many units to reject the Army's controversial M9 pistol — the license-built version of the Beretta 92. The SEALs dumped the Beretta after a catastrophic slide failure cost one man several teeth. Current pistols include SIG-Sauers, H&Ks and Colt M1911s. For long range shooting, the SEALs use match-grade M14 7.62mm rifles, Remington 700s or Barrett or McMillan .50in calibre sniper rifles. Night vision equipment is very important since so much of their work is carried out under cover of darkness: the SEALs are known to use AN/PVS-7 night vision goggles and AN/PVS-4 night sights.

For waterborne infiltration, the SEALs use Zodiac F-470 rubber boats that can carry seven men. Powered by outboard motor, these are very low and difficult to detect. Other boats include the 36ft (11m) fibreglass *Sea Fox* special warfare craft for high speed coastal raiding. Instead of normal SCUBA gear, the SEALs use closed-circuit systems that leave no tell-tale bubbles. For long distance underwater travel, the SEALs use Swimmer Delivery Vehicles: the Mk6 carries four divers while the Mk9 carries two. These are operated from two ex-nuclear missile submarines of the Ethan Allen class.

During the Gulf War, SEAL teams inside Kuwait and Iraq were racing around the desert in 80mph (129km/h) Fast Attack Vehicles (FAVs). These $50,000 dune buggies are adapted from an off-road racing vehicle and, equipped with M60 machine guns, M19 40mm grenade launchers and AT-4 anti-tank rockets, they are a spectacular addition to the SEALs' arsenal. SEAL FAVs were the first Allied military vehicles to enter Kuwait City.

Uniforms

The SEALs use modified US combat uniforms of whatever camouflage pattern is appropriate to their operational area.

Right: Static line parachute training for men of a Naval Special Warfare Unit based at Subic Bay, Philippines.

Below: Taking part in an exercise off the coast of California, a SEAL member departs his Zodiac F-470 low-profile rubber boat at the start of an underwater training exercise.

OTHER SUPER-VALUE MILITARY GUIDES IN THIS SERIES

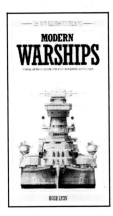

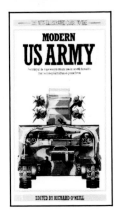

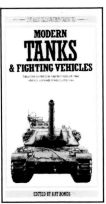

OTHER ILLUSTRATED MILITARY GUIDES AVAILABLE SOON.

Modern Attack Aircraft
Aircraft Markings
Modern US Fighters and Attack Aircraft
Modern US Navy
Modern Sub-Hunters

★ Each title has 160 fact-filled pages
★ Each is colorfully illustrated with hundreds of action photographs and technical drawings
★ Each contains concisely presented data and accurate descriptions of major international weapons systems
★ Each title represents tremendous value for money

If you would like further information on any of our titles please write to:
Publicity Department (Military Division), Salamander Books Ltd.,
129-137 York Way, London N7 9LG, United Kingdom.